OSTEOARTHRITIS

A step-by-step success story to encourage others to help themselves*

Fred L. Savage, P. Eng., BASc

* The original title was: <u>OSTEOARTHRITIS - How I learned to Live with It</u>.

The subtitle has been changed to emphasize the basic purpose of the book. There have been no changes in the contents since the first book was published.

Copyright © 1987 Fred L. Savage, P. Eng.

No part of this publication may be reproduced or transmitted in any form or by any means, electronic or mechanical, including photocopy, recording or any information storage and retrieval system now known or to be invented, without permission in writing from the author, except by a reviewer who wishes to quote brief passages in connection with a review written for inclusion in a magazine, newspaper or broadcast.

Canadian Cataloguing in Publication Data

ISBN   0 - 9693053 - 1 - 1

First printing:	200 copies	December, 1987
Second printing:	500 copies	February, 1988

With subtitle: How I Learned to Live With it

Third printing:	1000 copies	September, 1988

With subtitle: A Step-by-step Success Story to Encourage Others to Help Themselves

Printing by Fotoprint Ltd., Victoria, B. C.

Published in Canada by

Fred L. Savage Consulting
1230 Palmer Road,
Victoria, B. C.,
V8P 2H7

Telephone: (604) 382-8366

Text was developed on a Macintosh 512K computer with MacWrite software using Bookman font.   Master pages were laser printed by Camera Ready Graphics.

To my wife, Patricia,

who urged me to contact the Arthritis Centre before it was too late for effective treatment of my osteoarthritis, my deep appreciation for her understanding during my worst miseries.

To the physiotherapists of the Victoria Arthritis Centre,

who helped me and who were the first to show me that there were other ways and means of treating osteoarthritis, my appreciation for the treatment and for the knowledge which they imparted.

My thanks also to:

Dr. G. May, medical doctor
Dr. M. Marquette, naturopathic physician
Dr. D. Harwijne, doctor of chiropractic
Helen Jarvis, certified Trager® practitioner
Frank Roberts, president, OBUS Forme Ltd.
Ross McPhail, representative, Nike Canada

AUTHOR'S NOTE

This book has been written for informational purposes only and is in no way intended to substitute advice from a doctor or to replace the services of a physician, physiotherapist or chiropractor.

The Arthritis Society has requested that I ensure the reader is aware of the following excerpt from its review of this book:

> Much of the information contained in this book is personal, subjective, and unsubstantiated. There should be no indication of an endorsement from The Arthritis Society anywhere in this book.

No endorsement has been asked for or implied anywhere in this book.

I do not claim to be an expert. I am simply relating the particulars of my own experiences, which include roughly 12 hours of treatment at the Victoria Arthritis Centre, in trying to overcome continuing discomforts of my osteoarthritis.

Any application of my own personal methods as set forth in the following pages is at the reader's discretion and sole risk. What works for me may not work for others. After all, another person's remedies often do not work for me.

I recommend that he or she contact their doctor first and, if not automatically referred to an Arthritis Centre, to ask for such a referral.

My hope is that others with osteoarthritis will be encouraged by this book to:
- change their lifestyle,
- seek advice from the experts,
- question those experts,
- work out their own solutions for their discomfort,
- learn to <u>understand</u> how to live with the osteoarthritis.

I received help from:
- a medical doctor
- physiotherapists,
- a naturopathic physician,
- a chiropractor,
- a certified Trager ® practitioner.

Each of the above persons in his or her own way introduced me to a brand new way of living and methods of relaxation, all of which helped me reduce my pain and stiffness to more comfortable levels. I am very grateful for their help.

ACKNOWLEDGEMENTS

I wish to thank the following organizations for permitting me to use their registered trade (service) marks and information from their published pamphlets, books, etc.

These materials are included in the book because I believe that they help a person to develop an understanding of the problems of pain and arthritis, to learn how pain and stiffness may be reduced on one's own initiative and to maintain, even enhance, the positive results which one has achieved.

Arthritis Foundation

Comment made by Dr. F. McDuffie on the relationship between food poisoning and reactive arthritis as shown in item 4, page 64. This was noted in a newspaper clipping (source unknown) which was sent by a friend from Nevada. Item confirmed by Dr. F. McDuffie.

Nike, Inc.

Excerpts from the book Walk On, the description of methods of walking, page 20, copy of the illustrations describing the design of walking and running shoes, reference 9, page 72.

Obus Forme Ltd.

The drawing of an orthopaedic seat and backrest as shown on page 22. Details of the seat's functions from Obus Forme's advertising materials, as noted in ref. 5, page 69.

The Arthritis Society

Excerpts from <u>Grim Statistics</u>, Arthritis News, Summer 1986, page 2, as noted on page 1. Quotations from the Arthritic Information Series, <u>The Arthritis Society</u>, <u>What It Is and What It Does Across Canada</u>, as noted in ref. 3, pages 67 and 68.

The Orthotic Group Inc.

The information on faulty foot mechanics and the description of prescription orthotics from The Orthotic Group advertising materials, as noted in ref. 6, page 70.

The Trager[®] Institute

Use of the words Trager ®, Trager work, Mentastics [sm], use of the such descriptive words as "feel right", "feel light" on pages iv, 36 and 37, Dr. Milton Trager's quotation in ref. 7, page 71.

TRAGER ® is a registered service mark and MENTASTICS [sm] is a service mark of the Trager Institute. These service marks are used with permission of the Trager Institute.

FOREWORD

In July 1985 because of pains and stiffness my doctor had x-rays taken of my hands, knees and hips. When he diagnosed osteoarthritis, I looked for reading material on it but found that:

- while there were a number of books on arthritis and one on rheumatoid arthritis, Arthritis and Exercise[1], there was not one specifically written about osteoarthritis.

- the word, formed from (bone) **osteo + arthritis** (joint inflammation), was not even listed in Webster's dictionary.

I now realize how little was, and is, known about osteoarthritis.

- Some doctors call it a "degenerative bone disease"[3].
- One doctor writes it is not a disease or a terrible infection, it is simply pain from "inflammation caused by wear and tear"[2].
- Most seem to agree there is a "lack of an effective remedy"[3].

Other persons, who have contacted me recently, have attributed physical damage as the main cause of their osteoarthritis:

- One younger person said she has it in a knee from a skiing accident; another has it in her back from whiplash.
- Others attribute it to an injury from falling, heavy lifting, physical strain, etc. when muscles, ligaments, tendons, or cartilage have been damaged.

After the short physiotherapy period at the Arthritis Centre it became obvious to me that there was a lot more that I had to learn and do if my condition were to be improved:

- Some form of hands-on manipulation of my joints and muscles seemed most necessary for effective relief.
- Relaxing as well as strengthening exercises were required.
- There was no apparent reason for some of my discomfort.

Over a period of 30 months I investigated and tried many ways which I thought might help me improve my condition:

- diet, clothing, shoes, chairs, mattresses, posture, orthopaedic seats and backs, orthotics, body mechanics, methods of walking and exercising, Trager ® bodywork, etc.

With the help of others and through hard work and perseverance, I found ways which reduced my pains and stiffness.

I was introduced to Trager ® bodywork. I learned that the normal movement of my joints and muscles may be blocked by instinctive reactions protecting old areas of injury. I started to ask myself while moving or exercising:

does it feel right? lighter? freer? more mobile?

Then I included the relaxed, easy and coordinated movements of Trager Mentastics[sm] in my exercising.

I am still learning. Nothing remains the same. One improvement always seems to lead to other areas of need. For example, my daily walking program, through the period from Nov. '85 to this date, improved because:

1. Arthritis Centre exercises helped me resume walking,
2. Nike heel-cushioned jogging shoes made walking easier,
3. Orthotics removed developing knee and hip aches,
4. Nike's book <u>Walk On</u> showed me how to walk correctly,
5. Walking backwards up hills strengthened leg muscles,
6 Trager ® bodywork established new leg and hip freedom,
7. Mentastic[sm] walking movements eased leg and hip joints.

Sufferers from osteoarthritis need proper advice, help and encouragement, all of which is sometimes difficult to obtain.

Many people are unable to have the benefits of the Arthritis Centre facilities simply because :
- the Centres may be crowded or are not close to their homes,
- the treatment services may be limited by lack of funding, time, staff and space.

<u>Individuals should develop their own daily self-help.</u>

It is my opinion that one can not rely solely on others for help in improving their health. Medical costs are very high, health plan benefits may not apply to treatments and no other individual ever truly understands another's pain and condition.

I hope that this book encourages people to try and help themselves, to work actively towards reducing their own osteoarthritis discomfort.

Fred L. Savage, P. Eng.
(revised January, 1988)

CONTENTS

Introduction: some facts and statistics 1

Learning How to Live with Osteoarthritis 2
    Seven requirements for more comfort 3

Aches and Pains
    How osteoarthritis pain affects me 4
    How I cause pain for myself 4
    Soothing my aches and pains 4
        (A) Stiffness and pain in the hip 5
        (B) Pain radiating down my leg 6
        (C) Knee pains 6
        (D) Aches and pains in my hands and fingers 7
    Rest periods 7
    Some activities I avoid because of pain 8
    Ultra sound treatment and my osteoarthritis 8

The Need for a Proper Diet
    I am what I eat 9
    The essentials of our diet 10
    Vitamins 10

Less Aches and Pains, Warm or Cool
    Wearing apparel 11
    Blankets and mattress covers 12

Walking on Air
    Easing the foot down properly 13
    The modern jogging shoe 13
    What type of shoe is best? 14
    New walking problems 15
    Orthotics 15

Just Plain Walking
    Proper clothing and shoes 16
    Loosening up, ready for the walk 16
    Flat or hilly terrain, walking backwards 18
    Rest breaks 19
    General 20
    The Nike book "Walk On" 20

Chairs and Mattresses
    More leg and hip pains 21
    Sitting pretty 22
    Problems with soft chairs 23
    Problems with soft mattresses 23

Using the Body Properly
    On stairs and ramps 24
    When lifting and moving objects 25
    When kneeling 26

Posture
    In a sitting positon 28
    In a sleeping position 29
        Taking care as to how I get up. 30
    In a standing position 30
        Sweeping, vacuuming, raking. 31

House and Garden
    House tips 32
    Garden tips 33
        Types of equipment we use 34
        Wheelbarrow handle modification 34
        We always pull equipment 34
    I quit before I become tired 35

The Trager ® Experience 36

Exercises
    My reasons for exercising 37
    Tailoring the exercises to my needs 37
    Exercises and my back 38
    Hydrotherapy 38
    My approach to exercising 38
    The exercises which I do 39
    Frequency with which I do the exercises 39
    Exercises nos. 1 to 33 (for back, hips, legs, shoulders) 41
    Exercises I do for my fingers 57
    Exercises I do for my neck 58
    A note for back pain sufferers 61

Looking back a few years
    Knowing what I know now 62
    An objective look at my problems 62
        A) In the beginning. 62
        B) The discomfort caused by my lack of knowledge 63
        C) Hoping for the great cure-all. 63
        D) How about the individual's responsibility? 63

After all this, what do I recommend? 64

Equipment I use 65

References 67

INTRODUCTION: some facts and statistics

<u>Grim Statistics</u>, an Arthritis News article[3], presented a disturbing picture of the arthritis problem:

- arthritis is a leading cause of productivity loss,
- 16% of Canadians have some form of arthritis,
- 48.4% of those over 65 have it, mainly in the form of osteoarthritis,
- improvement is needed in public and medical education,
- researchers report that arthritic people drift away from their doctor and medication.

Dr. B. E. Koehler of The Arthritis Society, B. C. Division[4], estimates for a community of 100,000 population that the number of persons with osteoarthritis would be approximately 12,000 or 12 percent.

I learned that effective treatment was not simply a trip to the doctor's office and the pharmacy for medication.

> My body did not respond to ten weeks of medication.

> I was referred to The Arthritis Centre in Victoria. After eight sessions, three weeks of exercise and physiotherapy treatment, my condition improved in a fantastic manner.

> This success started me searching for means by which I could overcome other aches and pains which still bothered me from time to time.

What I discovered has enabled me to live with osteoarthritis in relative comfort without medication and, up to this date, without surgery.

<u>The wear and tear is still there.</u>

<u>I must accept the fact that it will be with me as long as I live.</u>

<u>To improve my condition, I changed my way of life</u>.

LEARNING HOW TO LIVE WITH OSTEOARTHRITIS

My osteoarthritis became noticeable in 1984.

- at first, my left hip would cramp and ache if I walked quickly for a distance of over a mile.

- by mid 1985, after walking half a city block, I would have to stop in order to ease the pain in both legs and hips. Going up or down stairs, driving a car, even lying in bed, was painful.

I now walk at least 2 km (1.2 miles) daily, climb stairs, drive a car without pain and have resumed many other activities. My condition has been improved with exercise and help from the following people.

July/85
: medical doctor
    - examination and x-rays
    - prescription for anti-inflammatory medicine
        Results:
        - diagnosis of osteoarthritis
        - referral to the Arthritis Centre

October/85
: physiotherapists (The Victoria Arthritis Centre)
    - therapy and hot pool workout
    - start of exercise program
        Results:
        - a general reduction of pain and stiffness
        - increased mobility

March/86
: naturopathic physician
    - nutrition discussion, new exercises
    - short period of diet supplements
        Results:
        - balanced diet, more effective weight control
        - improvement in general health

October/86
: orthopaedic device manufacturer[5]
    - Obus Forme ® seat and back supports
        Results:
        - relief of hip pain while sitting or driving

January/87
: chiropractor
    - discussion of posture, suggested exercises
    - foot imprints taken, orthotics[6] supplied
        Results:
        - reduced hip pain when walking or standing

May/87   certified Trager[7] ® practitioner
- gentle shaking, stretching, rhythmic rocking
- exercises for relaxing
    Results:
    - deep relaxation of muscles and joints

It was evident that my lack of attention to my physical needs over several years had caused the osteoarthritis to develop into a very unpleasant condition. Simply stated, I had neglected to maintain:

- a good range of motion with my joints,
- strong leg muscles to protect my knees and hips,

and to make matters much worse I had continually stressed my fingers, knees and hips with physical labour around the house and garden.

Seven requirements for more comfort

From my experiences, which I list in the following pages, I have concluded that all I really need, to live more comfortably with osteoarthritis, is the following:

1. **an exercise program, walking, outdoor activities**
2. **a balanced diet**
3. **orthopaedic seat and back supports, orthotics, foam mattress, firm chairs**
4. **correct posture, good body mechanics**
5. **proper clothing and footwear**
6. **if possible, a monthly Trager ® bodywork session**
7. **a minimum of overexertion, stress and fatigue**

In some books and articles relating to arthritis I read of marvelous "cures". One recommendation of using apple cider vinegar would have been too much for me because of the acidity but I tried three others which did not appear too outlandish or dangerous. I concluded that if a person deeply believed in the efficacy of the cure it might help.

I went back to my seven requirements as listed above.

ACHES AND PAINS

How osteoarthritis pain affects me

Pain is most frequent and persistent in my left hip area. Pain sometimes radiates from the hip down the side of the thigh to the shin of the leg.

There is a specific point of pain in the large indentation of the left hip. I can reduce this problem with exercises, orthotics, shoes, new ways of walking.

- By walking on the outside of my feet, one foot ahead of the other (see page 20).

- Or by pretending to kick a tin can, gently, idly, as Tom Sawyer might do on a hot summer day (Dr. Trager's Mentastics[sm], page 37).

Thumb and finger joints may ache occasionally but the pain is most easily remedied with finger execises.

Knee pain is minor, easily overcome by exercising.

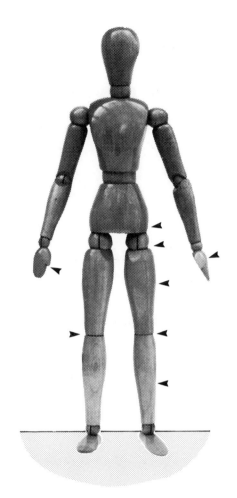

How I cause pain for myself

1. **excessive walking or exercising.**
2. **taking insufficient rest periods.**
3. **carrying, lifting or pushing objects.**
4. **sitting too long, sitting in soft chairs.**
5. **wearing incorrect clothing, shoes.**
6. **using too many or too few blankets on the bed.**
7. **lying on a mattress which has poor support.**
8. **eating incorrectly.**

Soothing my aches and pain

Medication, even the old standby acetylsalicylic acid, does not relieve my pains. Instead I use rest, exercises, methods of walking and avoid positions or conditions which cause pain.

(A) <u>Stiffness and pain in the hip</u>

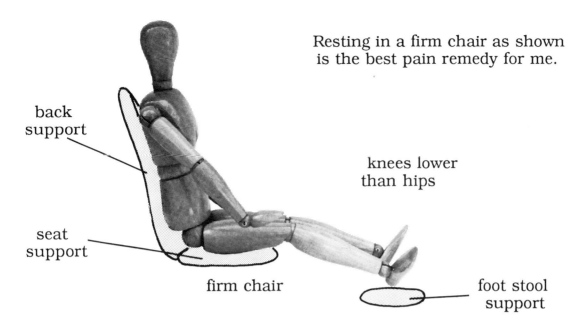

Resting in a firm chair as shown is the best pain remedy for me.

back support

knees lower than hips

seat support

firm chair

foot stool support

Another rest position is lying on my stomach on the floor. The floor supports the stomach better and prevents excessive arching of the back which may occur with mattress sag. An Arthritis Centre physiotherapist recommended trying this at least 10 minutes a day.

sometimes while in this position I rub the muscles in the area of the large indentation of the hips.

I have no strain if I keep my arms by my sides and my head turned sideways on the floor.

Sometimes I just "slump" and rest.

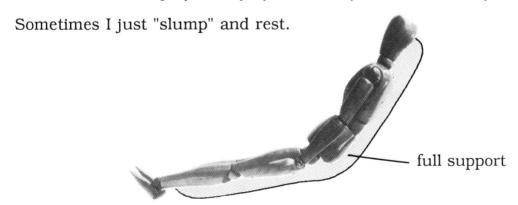

full support

Massaging muscles in a painful area also helps. I sometimes apply low heat (palm of my hand is often enough) or a cool object to a sore spot on a hot day. A hot or a cold compress works well for me.

(B) Pain radiating down my leg

Two areas where massage is efective in relieving leg pains for me are shown in the sketch on the right.

- the large indentation on the hip
- the lower half of the outside of the thigh

I relax the muscles and, massage for 30 seconds, rest and repeat as necessary.

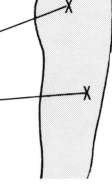

(C) Knee pains

I find that rotating my kneecaps gently 20 - 30 times daily keeps them loose and feeling fine.

The following has always proven a good remedy for slightly sore knees.

I place the right leg with its heel on a block and hang two ankle weights on the right knee which is kept straight. The left leg lies relaxed on the floor. I hold this position for 2 or 3 minutes and then change over to the left leg.

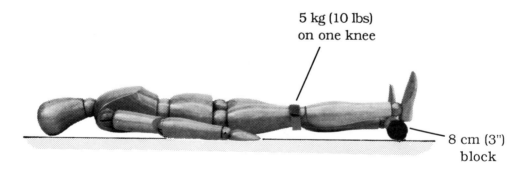

5 kg (10 lbs) on one knee

8 cm (3") block

Certain exercises at the start caused a slight lower back ache. The position shown at the top of next page (7) helped stop the pain.

I hang legs over arm of chair for a minute, rest and repeat.

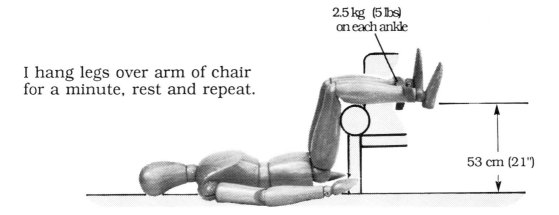

(D) Aches and pains in my hands and fingers

Too much carpentry, pulling weeds and roots in the garden, light shovelling, etc. will cause my finger muscles to stiffen and ache. Heavy gloves must be worn at all times to protect both hands and fingers.

The best "cure" for my finger aches is prevention. My fingers have not swollen or pained me over the past 18 months since I started to perform finger exercises on a regular daily basis. See pages 58, 59 and 60.

Rest periods

The Arthritis Centre recommended that I should ensure that I always took adequate rest periods and did not overtire myself.

I am continually amazed how quickly I can "bounce" back and feel refreshed if I stop and rest early enough. Some simple activities which tire and stress me are:

- **too much walking and exercising**
- **going up and down stairs**
- **sitting and standing**
- **holding one position too long**
- **any repetitive use of legs, hands and arms**

It is too easy to forget that rest periods are an important part of my present life, particularly when I become engrossed in an activity which may not appear to be physical and strenuous, for example, typing, writing, computer work, etc.

I should mention The Common Cold as it brings on a deeper tiredness now than ever in the past. It often creates arthritis-like aches, pain and stiffness in my back, hips and legs days before any of the cold symptoms appear. To combat a cold, I find that I need warmth, light food, vitamins, continued but lighter exercise, with lots of fluid and rest, rest and more rest.

Some activities I avoid because of pain

Pain can grind a person down and affect one's whole life. One has to adapt an attitude, a motto (taken from my engineering undergraduate years) of *illegitimi non carborundum*.

My program of daily exercise has definitely improved my physical condition. Stronger muscles have made it possible for me to enjoy light activities without pain and this has given me a lift.

Sports such as tennis are obviously too physically demanding. However, there are other less strenuous activities which I have to limit, others which I just can not do and will never do again.

> <u>Walking on a sloping beach or across uneven ground</u> - my knees and hips can not tolerate one foot being lower than the other for an extended period of time.
>
> <u>Bicycling</u> - this is much too strenuous for my knees joints.
>
> <u>Jogging</u> - a few hurried, jogger-like steps in a crosswalk quickly convinced me that jogging is painful. However, I believe that at my age the exercises and short walks keep my muscles in better shape than a jogging routine would.
>
> <u>Hiking</u> - a small amount is fine if the hills are such that I can walk up them backwards and this usually limits the hike to level and well defined gravel or paved paths. See page 18.

If an activity causes pain I **stop**, <u>investigate the reason for the pain</u> and either make some adjustment in what I am doing or avoid the action completely right now, and in the future.

Ultra sound treatment and my osteoarthritis

My experience with ultra sound treatment has been variable. When I put two ribs out of place I am sure that this treatment helped to ease the soreness and speed the recovery process.

However, when I had it applied in April/86 to my left hip, it aggravated the sensitive spot in that area and gave me no relief. The treatment did not seem right for my particular osteo-arthritis condition, it had a heating effect which obviously was not what I needed and I have not had it applied again.

This was a good illustration to me of how reactions may vary within my own body. In this respect it is easy to see why some people may gain relief in ways which are not effective for others.

THE NEED FOR A PROPER DIET

I am what I eat

In March/86, Dr. Marquette suggested that I try changing my diet, to increase the amounts of vegetables and to eat more fish.

I found this to be good advice and, in trying to practise it, I have become more aware of the value of proper food. However, the experts suggest that I am on unsound ground when I state my belief that, for better health and for reduction of discomfort,

a balanced diet is essential for people with osteoarthritis.

Instead they repeatedly emphasize that diet is not a cure for arthritis which I feel tends to play down the importance of diet. They also say that diet may not work for others as it does for me. I draw the reader's attention to the fourth item on page 64.

In my experience, a poor diet makes my osteoarthritis worse!

When I eat unwisely or eat too much, I add weight to my body which worn knee and hip joints must carry. Osteoarthritis makes it difficult enough for me to bend over, to put on my socks and shoes and tie the laces; I do not want to stretch around an oversized paunch as well.

Some foods definitely cause my joints and muscles to ache.

I have often blamed osteoarthritis when the real culprits for some of my aches have been food and drink. I associate anything acidic, e.g., tomatoes, dry wine, pickles, sauerkraut, orange juice, vinegars, etc. with increased discomfort.

I have trouble with stimulants, some spices and certain food additives and preservatives.

In this category I now place coffee, tea, chocolate, peppers (black, white and cayenne), tabasco, paprika, or any food which causes my body to heat up.

I try to avoid specific items in my diet because of the general feeling of unease which they cause, the fattening aspects of some, the aches which others cause. Some of these are:

> Rich desserts, sugar
> Alcohol, especially wines and beers with additives
> Coffee and strong tea, chocolate
> Hot spices, MSG, sodium salt
> Junk and processed foods

I learned about osteoarthritic joints in Arthritis Centre education sessions. Even with the most miraculous diet, I would conclude that a body could not repair this type of damage.

> I have no faith in quack diets. I can not help but feel that they are just so much rubbish; some of them make no sense at all. On the other hand, I see evidence that the balanced diet, with lots of bone and muscle building food and fibre, makes my body more efficient and helps it cope with my osteoarthritis.

The essentials of our diet

Dr. Marquette and others have recommended the following and we try to include them in our diet over the period of a week. Most important, they agree with us.

- **Cereals, multigrain, hot or cold**
- **Multigrain bread**
- **Milk, Yogurt, Cottage cheese,**
- **Raw fruit, very light on citrus fruits**
- **Raw and/or cooked fresh vegetables**
- **Small amounts of various nuts, raisins**
- **Minimal butter, no margarine**
- **Fish, eggs, small amounts of fowl, red meat, cheese**
- **Lots of fresh water**

When I slip up on my eating I know why parts of me hurt more!

Vitamins and other compounds

Up to late 1986 I felt that I needed certain vitamins, Niacin, C, D, etc., minerals and other compounds. I believe that they did me a lot of good during the first 18 months.

> When my exercises, diet, etc. began to take effect my new diet appeared to be sufficient for my needs. I use vitamin C when I have a cold. An acquaintance with arthritis uses raw wheat germ as an antidote, but, on my cereal, it just upsets my stomach.

Dr. Marquette recommended that I take two special compounds for three months to reduce swollen finger joints.

> My engineer's iron ring, trapped on my little finger for more than a year, came off easily after 6 weeks of taking these compounds. I have no idea whether this was coincidence or not but I do know that the swollen joints have never occured again.

LESS ACHES AND PAINS, STAY WARM OR COOL

Wearing apparel

My early thinking was that with osteoarthritis I should keep warm at all times, in fact, the warmer the better. However, I know now that being too warm is as painful as being cold.

Clothing made of fabrics such as wool, polyester, etc., which have a heating effect, may cause my legs and hips to ache if a room is too warm or a summer day is hot. It is similar to being cold, the only difference is the stiffness which cold causes.

Each time this occurred I would think my osteoarthritis had flared up again. Maybe it is my age of 66 but I could tolerate a wider range of temperatures two and a half years before the osteoarthritis became a noticeable problem.

I have learned to wear light, warm clothing which can be easily taken off or put back on to meet the changing conditions.

> In the late fall, winter and early spring I must wear long underwear and be ready to change into lighter clothing if the temperature rises.
>
> On hot days I need looser clothing, short pants, etc. to stay cool. I find temperatures over 32° C (90° F) cause hip pain and I may have to apply a cold compress to the hip area for a while.
>
> Gloves, hats, or scarves can help maintain a comfortable condition without overheating the whole body. Hands and head are surfaces by which I can effectively maintain my comfort levels. I cover them up or uncover them as the temperature demands.

I have learned to be constantly aware of temperature changes and to recognize quickly my body's reactions to them.

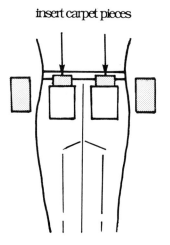

Two pieces of indoor/outdoor carpet, cut to fit inside my pants' back pockets, will insulate that area against cold or wind without affecting the rest of my body.

This provided me with a good illustration of how heat will cause aches. If I forget to remove the pieces when the temperature rises my hips start to ache and will continue to do so until the area is cool again.

If I sit in an air conditioned or drafty place where the ambient temperature is lower than 22° C (72° F) I can expect my left hip to ache. From my osteoarthritic point of view modern air conditioning in buildings and cars cools far below the comfort level.

Blankets and mattress covers

The Arthritis Centre recommended that we use light blankets when sleeping. I found this to be good advice.

From my experience two lightweight loom woven thermal blankets of 50% acrylic and 50% polyester are excellent covers. They are easily moved off or on to meet the changing temperatures in the room.

Because I have to be careful that my left hip does not get cold I often use one blanket full length on the bed and have the second blanket drawn up to my waist. In the summer I may only use a sheet with possibly a blanket just below the waist.

Normally I use the two thermal blankets and a sheep's wool mattress cover, as shown in the following sketch.

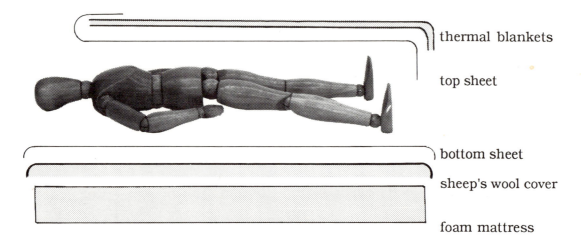

The sheep's wool mattress cover insulates me against the mattress preventing it from absorbing valuable heat from my body. This is similar to the old woodsman's trick of conserving his body heat with a heavy layer of blankets underneath him while he slept. Note that this wool cover may provide too much heat in hot weather particularly with a foam mattress.

Too much blanket and I am back to same pain-in-the-leg problem I have with clothing, the possibility of becoming overheated.

WALKING ON AIR

Easing the foot down softly

I learned in an Arthritis Centre education session that leg bones normally absorb a part of the shock which is caused when the heel strikes the ground but that this cushioning ability gradually reduces with age.

When the leg bones no longer absorb shock efficiently then the leg muscles have to be capable of providing more protection to the knee and hip joints. For persons with osteoarthritis if their muscles are in poor condition their joints take the shock load and are jarred, stressed and damaged further.

While exercising strengthens the leg muscles to handle the shock I find that this is not enough for me. I require cushioning systems which are built within the shoes to ensure my heel is eased into a softer landing as I walk.

The Arthritis Centre therapists recommended that I use jogging shoes which have built-in shock absorbers to cushion the striking shock.

The modern jogging shoe

The first jogging shoe which I tried was the Nike Air ® Epic and I thought that it was the best "walking" shoe that I had ever owned.

- The cushioning effect was like walking on air.
- Walking became a comfortable, enjoyable exercise for the first time in years.

This shoe had the recommended features of lace up, broad heel, firm heel cup, arch support, stability and cushioning insole.

I tried another shoe and found, after a few weeks of use, that:

- it did not provide a firm enough side support for the heel,
- it did not control my foot's tendency to rock and roll,
- it did not have effective cushioning.

I check my choice of shoe carefully otherwise I may spend a lot of money and end up without the proper equipment.

WHAT TYPE OF SHOE IS BEST?

I have bought shoes which I can not wear because, after I wore them for several weeks, I found them unsuitable for my way of walking. They caused leg aches and their lack of stability, side support, etc. made my walking uncomfortable.

> The problem of these shoes arose when I had to replace the shoes which had been first recommended to me and found that the model had been discontinued.
>
> As far as I know there is no mass produced shoe made especially for a person with osteoarthritis. I have had to recognize that most on-the-shelf shoes are made with relatively healthy bodies in mind, not bodies such as mine suffering worn and torn joints.
>
> With my osteoarthritis I had to adapt to what was available.

I tried shoes made especially for walkers but they seemed to fall short of my personal requirements. The shoe which suited me best was a running shoe, the Nike Air ® Support, with its features of extra cushioning, good stability and heel support.

The Nike book <u>Walk On</u>[8] has a good section on walking and running shoe design. It discusses the important differences of heel strike, the need for more flexibility and thinner soles in walking shoes.

> I have taken copies of the illustrations in the Nike book <u>Walk On</u> which show the differences between walking and running shoes and have shown them in Reference 9, page 72.

I have not put the Nike Air ® Walker to a full test yet, preferring to stay with what I can buy off the shelf from the local Nike retailer who is always available for advice and who understands my problem.

New walking problems

I wore my first Nike-Air ® shoes constantly for six months with no problems and then attended an hour long meeting wearing regular leather shoes. The pain in my left hip was severe.

At the time the reaction seemed rather extreme and I thought that it was possibly related to another developing problem; namely, the way my left hip would start to ache as I walked and the left foot struck the ground.

Orthotics[6]

Dr. Harwijne diagnosed "pronation" meaning that my ankles sloped inward, distorting relationships between leg joints and feet. Longitudinal and transverse arches of my feet were flat.

To correct these conditions she made cast imprints of my feet which a laboratory used to design biomechanical orthotic devices which "captured" the best functioning position of my feet.

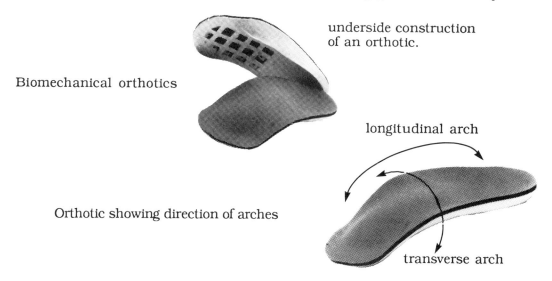

Biomechanical orthotics

underside construction of an orthotic.

longitudinal arch

transverse arch

Orthotic showing direction of arches

After I had worn these devices for one week my hip pain disappeared. A pronation wedge was added to the heel of my left orthotic about three months later.   Results were excellent.

I wear a sports model orthotic which has a thin cushioning layer on the top. This works well with my regular leather shoes and even they are now comfortable over a short period of time.

JUST PLAIN WALKING

Proper clothing and shoes

I noted recently on a TV program that the cool, damp west coast weather is said to bother persons with rheumatism. The dampness does not seem to bother my osteoarthritis.

I find that if I dress warmly, never allowing any part of my body to become chilled, then our damp winter months are not a problem. It is the strong winds with temperatures below 16° C (60° F) which create the worst conditions for me.

When walking during the late fall, winter and early spring, I wear long underwear, warm and lightweight clothing, a down parka, hat, gloves, scarf and heavier socks. When a wind is blowing, I wear a knee length coat.

In warmer weather I dress carefully to avoid being too warm. Hot weather aches develop so suddenly that I do not at first attribute their cause to my body's overheating. A change of clothing or cooler weather will change my condition quickly.

I always wear jogging shoes and the orthotics when walking.

Loosening up, ready for the walk

I am one of those people whose muscles tense with walking so it is important that I loosen up first. These exercises help me:

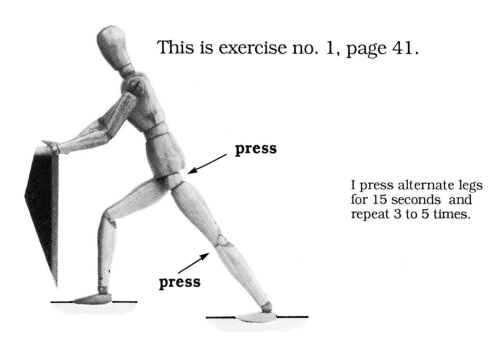

This is exercise no. 1, page 41.

I press alternate legs for 15 seconds and repeat 3 to 5 times.

Exercise 3 C
page 42

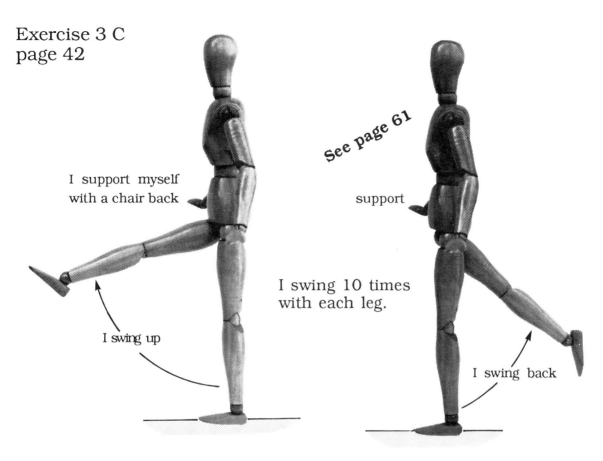

I support myself with a chair back

I swing up

See page 61

support

I swing 10 times with each leg.

I swing back

I also walk in this manner.

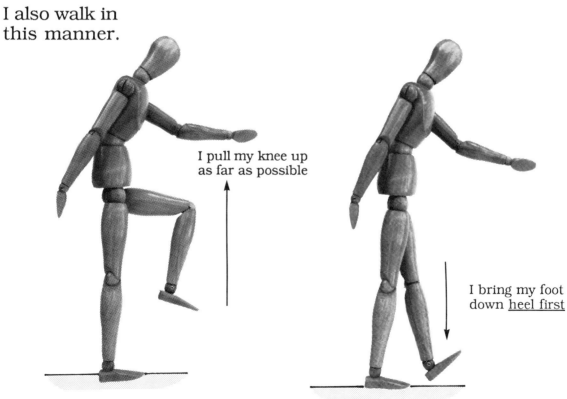

I pull my knee up as far as possible

I bring my foot down <u>heel first</u>

I walk forward - 25 paces.

I walk sideways for 20 paces each way to loosen up the hip area:

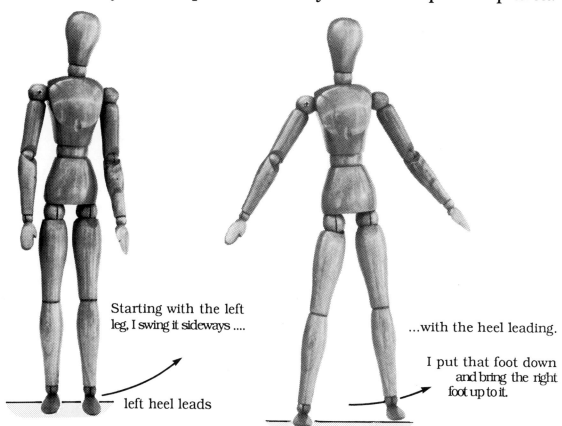

Starting with the left leg, I swing it sideways ....

— left heel leads

...with the heel leading.

I put that foot down and bring the right foot up to it.

Flat or hilly terrain, walking backwards

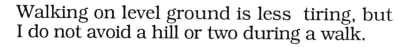

Walking on level ground is less tiring, but I do not avoid a hill or two during a walk.

<u>On a hill I try to walk backwards</u>, hoping that people do not become too curious of what I am doing.

Walking backwards on any rising slope is easier for me and I find it excellent exercise for the buttock and thigh muscles.

One acquaintance said that it was the only way he could "walk" along parts of the Great Wall of China.

I keep legs straight, rise on toes to adjust for slope

Rest breaks

The Arthritis Centre recommended that I stop any activity if an ache became noticeable and then rest.

After walking a while I sit down on a bench, <u>push back</u> until my buttocks and back are fully supported and relax for as long as I wish.

While still sitting I may follow up with this version of exercise 25, page 53 as shown on the left.

Sometimes I feel the need for a little more loosening up in my hip area and use:

- exercise 11, page 46, as shown in the bottom left hand corner,

- or, exercise 13, page 47, as below.

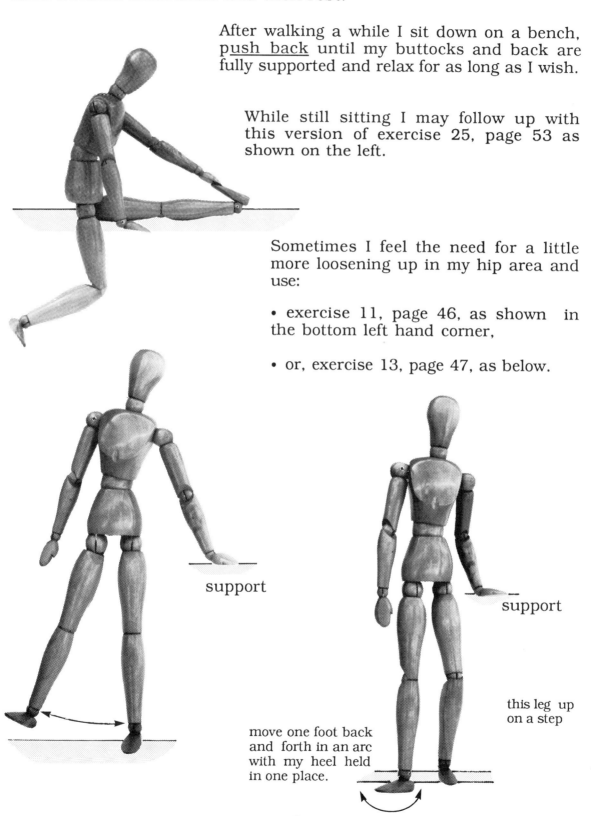

support

move one foot back and forth in an arc with my heel held in one place.

support

this leg up on a step

- 19 -

General

I enjoy walking now and this is a complete reversal from my attitude of two to three years ago. I expect to enjoy it more in the future with the help of the book Walk On [8](and see below).

I have walked 3 km (1.8 mi.) on an ideal day, a warm 22^0 C (72^0F) with no winds. My overall time with three rest breaks was 50 minutes. I estimate my average distance is 2 km (1.2 mi.) but I never try to set records or force myself to walk faster or farther.

I do not walk on those days when I know that later in the day I will be cutting the lawn or doing some other physical work. There is no need for additional exercise which could tire me and then cause more wear and tear damage.

The NIKE book "Walk On"[8]

Walk-On warns that the information it contains "is meant for healthy people". I respect that notice.

With my osteoarthritis I will never be a strider but I can benefit from a slower pace of walking if I know how to walk correctly. I have learned a lot about walking from Walk On and have tried some of its recommendations such as:

- rocking my pelvis to firm the buttocks and strengthen the lower abdominals.
- crossing my feet while I walk to get more mobility in my hips.
- walking on the outside of my feet to establish a better relationship between foot and leg.
- walking on my heels to strengthen shin muscles and stretch my hamstrings.
- taking small steps to loosen up feet and ankles.
- walking in figure eights to stretch the hips.
- rolling shoulders to loosen muscles.
- looking back over a shoulder to strengthen back muscles.
- even, breathing away sore legs!

There is also information on such items as: height/body weight chart, pelvic tilt test, pulse counting, self massage, walk breaks, daily walking cycles and much more.

In my opinion this book is a valuable guide for osteoarthritis sufferers who need information on how to walk correctly and who wish to get the most benefit from this type of exercise.

CHAIRS AND MATTRESSES

More leg and hip pains

My condition improved steadily for 8 to 9 months and then, whenever I sat in a soft chair or drove a car, my left leg and hip would start to ache severely.

In August, 1986, I attended a church wedding and was concerned that I would be sitting for an hour or more. It was a time when I had to move about and stretch between even short periods of sitting.

When I stood up at the end of the service it was a real surprise to find that I had no pain or stiffness.

I attributed this to the hard wooden pew and the thin cushion.

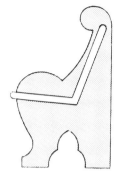

I tried a piece of plywood and a thin cushion on various seats but the results were so variable it was obvious that the softness of the seat was not the sole cause of my discomfort.

I noticed that I always "sank" into car, aircraft, bus and theatre seats or soft chairs. My knees would be well above my buttocks and I literally "sagged".

A small airline pillow or a rolled up sweater placed on the seat as shown reduced my "sag" and gave me some relief from this sitting pain.

Further experimentation showed that the slope of the seat and the angle of the back was critical for my comfort

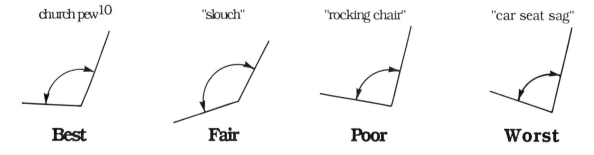

The above sketches show how certain seat types affect me from comfort to . . . . severe discomfort.

Sitting pretty

In October 1986 I discovered the Obus Forme ® orthopaedic seat and back supports[5]. I felt the benefit of this combination immediately I used them.

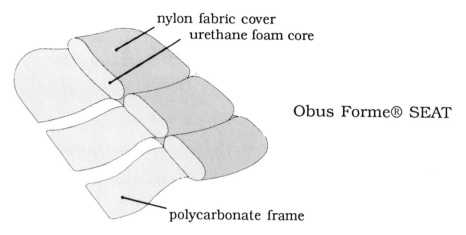

When I saw the Obus Forme ® illustration and description (below), showing the relative position of the sitting bones, I understood why I had trouble with soft seats and chairs.

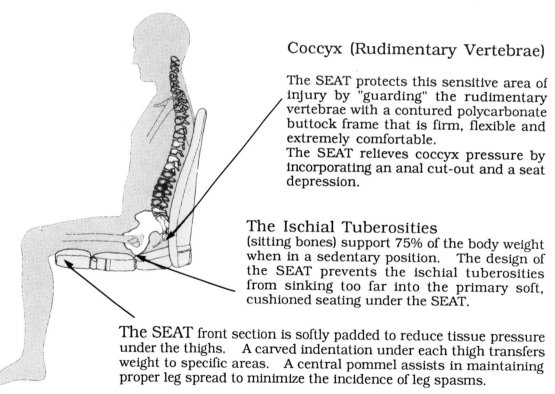

These supports are light and easy to carry. I use the SEAT only when we go to friends' homes, theatres, restaurants, etc. but use both supports at home or when driving or travelling.

Problems with soft chairs

Two years ago when rising from a soft or low chair I used to feel like a bent pin, unable to straighten up or stand erect properly. I would have to struggle, stress my knees badly, in getting up from the low sitting position of most upholstered chairs.

All this has changed with the use of the Obus Forme ® SEAT and careful chair selection.

In our home we replaced chair cushions with better foam and strengthened seat springs. When visiting I now look for firmer, higher or wooden chairs and use the Obus Forme ® SEAT. There are further sitting details on pages 28 and 29.

Problems with soft mattresses

I was very remiss in not investigating my mattress requirements at an early date. When I finally changed from a coil mattress and box spring to a foam mattress I slept better.

A quarter to a third of my life is spent sleeping. In this respect, a poor mattress could easily have a negative effect.

My foam mattress never causes aches or stiffness. I use a 6" deep U28 foam mattress, of medium firmness, laid on a wood slat base. The foam compresses and "pushes" back to give the firm support for all parts of my body. It breathes and does not cause heat to buildup to an uncomfortable level.

I have learned that a mattress should be firm, not hard, and should provide both vertical and lateral support.

Uniform, vertical support to all areas in contact with the body protects such pressure points as the shoulders and hips.

Lateral support reduces any quick and irregular sideways movement.

Soft mattresses and poor box springs make travelling a hazard. Some mattresses may feel firm but, after a few hours, they depress slightly under my hips to wake me up with hip pain.

I have had to slip the Obus Forme ® BACK under me (in a $90.00 per night hotel room) to get a better sleep. The BACK was never designed for this use but it helps me in temporary situations.

Unless the modern air mattress, with the new "air coils", is over-inflated to a hard, almost unyielding surface, I find that it will gradually depress and cause me pain.

USING THE BODY PROPERLY

On stairs and ramps

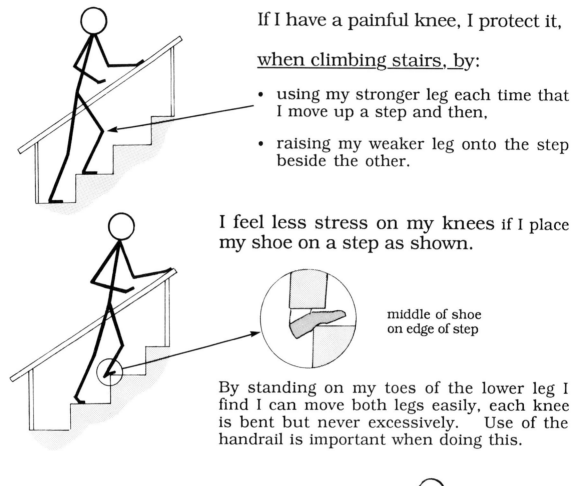

If I have a painful knee, I protect it,

<u>when climbing stairs, by</u>:

- using my stronger leg each time that I move up a step and then,

- raising my weaker leg onto the step beside the other.

I feel less stress on my knees if I place my shoe on a step as shown.

middle of shoe on edge of step

By standing on my toes of the lower leg I find I can move both legs easily, each knee is bent but never excessively. Use of the handrail is important when doing this.

<u>when walking down stairs by</u>:

- moving down one stair at a time and,

- lowering my weak leg first with its knee joint only slightly bent.

This means that when I shift from one leg to the other on stairs the weaker leg is <u>only slightly bent</u> when it takes my full weight.

I have commented in the sections on walking and gardening that I prefer to walk backwards up a slope.

- I find it is easier to walk this way if I keep my knees slightly bent. My leg muscles certainly feel this exercise.

- There is a positive response, a feeling of good tone and condition, in the muscles of the buttock area as I walk backwards.

When lifting and moving objects

Back Stress

Lifting in this position, i.e. with the back, causes serious back problems.

Lifting is difficult with osteoarthritis.

This is an approved stance for lifting if the body is healthy with strong leg muscles and sound joints.

<u>I can not use it because of the possibility of severe knee and hip strain.</u>

There are many ways to move an object but if I **must** move an object by lifting:

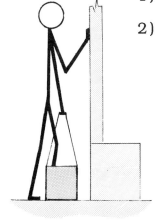

1) I make a sling to lift the load.

2) Brace myself against a wall or a door jamb.

3) I keep my knees slightly bent, back straight, I lift object up to a new level with my arm muscles.

Picking up an object, twisting my body with the load and then carrying it any distance is an act of utter stupidity on my part.

If the object is cumbersome or is over 5 kg (10 lb), I find it best to move it mechanically. This protects and saves my hands, knees, hips, neck and back for more enjoyable activities.

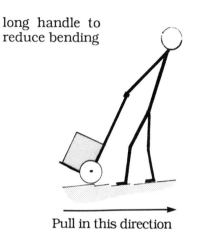

long handle to reduce bending

Pull in this direction

I am able to pull a handcart with a load of 50 kg (100 lbs) without any ill effects to my joints.

However, if I push a handcart with a 50 kg load, my left hip and knee joints will pain me.

I carry only the lightest objects up stairs.

I am lucky because we live in a single storey house with few stairs.

I have learned not to carry more than 5 kg (10 lbs) at any time to avoid knee and hip stress.

If I had to move heavier objects, under 25 kg (50 lbs), I would use a handcart with at least 20 cm (8") diameter wheels.

For large, cumbersome or heavy objects I simply ask for help.

When kneeling

Some experts frown on kneeling, but sometimes it is unavoidable. The trick, I believe, is to do it carefully and use commonsense, I prepare myself for getting down and **the gettingup**.

Two important items must be in place before I bend to kneel:

1. a urethane foam pad, U-30 density, to kneel upon,
2. a stool or kneeler-stool to lean on so that my arms carry part of my weight.

I use the Corrie Easi-Kneeler Stool[11] which may be used either as a stool or a kneeler.

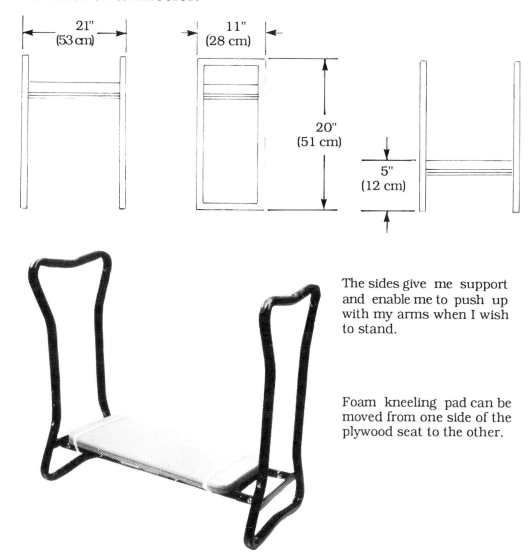

The sides give me support and enable me to push up with my arms when I wish to stand.

Foam kneeling pad can be moved from one side of the plywood seat to the other.

With this or similar equipment I do not have trouble when I kneel.

> Using one's hands and arms to lower to or raise from a kneeling position makes it impossible to lift an object while bending down or getting up.

> This prevents any possibility of overloading the knee when the joint is in an angular and most vulnerable position.

POSTURE

In a sitting position

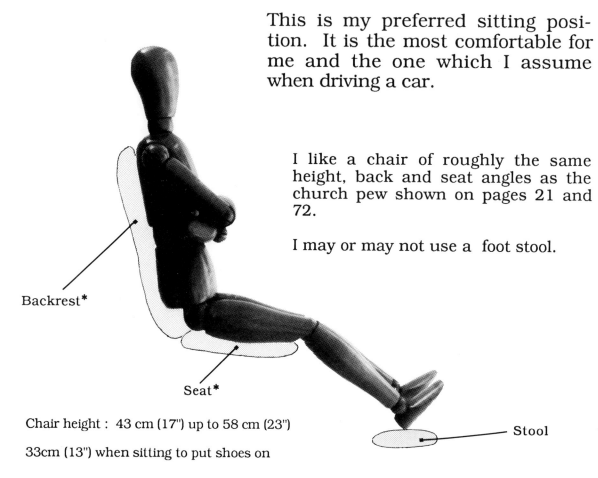

This is my preferred sitting position. It is the most comfortable for me and the one which I assume when driving a car.

I like a chair of roughly the same height, back and seat angles as the church pew shown on pages 21 and 72.

I may or may not use a foot stool.

Chair height : 43 cm (17") up to 58 cm (23")

33cm (13") when sitting to put shoes on

* Obus Forme ® gives me firm contured support exactly where I need it.

For me, a comfortable sitting position must have:

- a firm primary cushion, strong springs, a reasonable slope to the chair's back and seat and an orthopaedic seat and backrest to provide positive, contured support.

- a seat height of at least 43 cm (17"), including sag, to lower the stress on the knees when moving off the chair; to help maintain a more comfortable leg, hip, back relationship when sitting, i.e., to keep my legs lower than or level with my hips.

- a foot stool, as needed, to ensure a comfortable position.

I do not bend my knees and place my feet under a chair while sitting because this position causes my knees to ache.

I get up from to time to time, stretch, walk around or do something else to avoid the buildup of stiffness. When I am driving a car, I have to:

- sit back from the steering wheel,
- extend my legs (knees only slightly bent),
- use Obus Forme ® seat and back supports,
- lay a small pillow on the seat if it is low or has too much sag.

This is also the only way that I can remain comfortable in any similar seat such as is used in aircraft, bus, theatres, etc.

I blame the poor design of modern furniture and seats for the sitting discomfort with which many of us are faced today.

Most upholstered furniture looks right; it has the correct seat slope and angle of the back <u>as long as it is not in use</u>.

I can not sit on them and be comfortable without the orthopaedic supports, etc. I have noted with surprise that most people with sore backs choose the same higher, nearly upright, firmer, and, if they are available, wooden chairs as I do.

I tried out a computer or desk chair as is shown on the left.

I believe that it would tend to make a person sit with a better posture. It was fine for my hips, but the bent knees would ache within minutes.

It was also difficult to leave the chair without stressing the knees.

In a sleeping position

With a foam mattress I am able to sleep in almost any position but with other mattresses I am forced to lie on my left side:

right knee bent

left leg straight, left hip join t (my bad hip) straight

I find that I turn over onto my stomach during my sleep. It is a comfortable position for me although it is not recommended because of back stress.

When early exercises made my back sore, I tried the following sleeping positions but they bothered both hip and knee joints.

- Lying on my back with the knees elevated.
- Lying on my side and curling up in a ball.
- Lying on my side with a pillow between the thighs.

Taking care as to how I get up

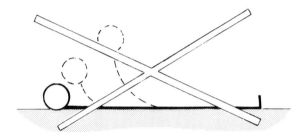

In the past I have stressed my neck and back by lifting my head and then torso to raise myself from the bed or floor.

The method I use now is to roll onto one side, pushing myself over with one bent leg, so that I can get into position to push up with my arms into a sitting position.

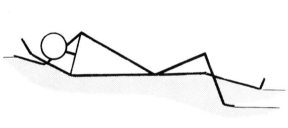 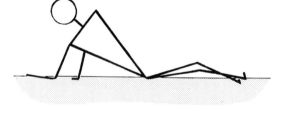

roll over   push with bent leg   push up with arms

In a standing position

When on a walk just standing still for a few minutes is restful, but it is a different matter to stand and work in one position for longer periods of time.

I try to stand in a comfortable position with my knees slightly bent. Fatigue will ultimately set in and muscles will tire and ache.

A stool which is high enough to provide a good sitting/working height is one remedy.

I find that a foot rest is often better. I alternate one foot with the other reducing muscle stress effectively.

My neck, shoulders, back, hips, knees and hands become stressed when I stand and perform sweeping, vacuuming or raking movements.

In August, 1987, I went along with a suggestion that by bending my knees slightly while doing the above work, or my exercises, I would strengthen my leg muscles, force them carry more of the load and, consequently, reduce the stress on my joints.

> I thought that it was a good idea but I should have known better. It was a mistake. My knee joints became quite painful and it took about two weeks to bring them back to their previous condition. I keep my knees as straight as is practical now.

I eliminate needless drudgery or stress by using muscle saving devices. I would suggest that there are number of these devices on the market which can help arthritis sufferers keep active.

> Large sweeping jobs, which involve so much repetitive movement, were difficult for me but now I "sweep" the driveway and walks with a leaf blower.

> The big problem of raking and gathering leaves has been resolved with the leaf blower, a plastic ground sheet and handcart. I take less time to do this chore than ever before.

> Pushing a conventional vacuum is the worst action for my leg joints. Someone recommended a stance "of a lunging fencer with an immobile back". When I tried this I felt as if I were on the receiving end of a sword thrust to the hip.

> Vacuuming only a small section of floor every day helps. My strong shop vacuum is excellent for the bigger jobs as I am able to <u>pull</u> the vacuum head and it is good body action for me. This type of vacuum is also useful in the garden.

HOUSE AND GARDEN

I plan my activities. I stop before I become tired. I leave what is undone for the next day.

Repetitive or physical work is interrupted by rest breaks. I shift the work load between different muscles so that no part of the body is unduly stressed.

If I am on my feet I wear jogging shoes and orthotics.

House tips

Sweeping and vacuuming is discussed on the previous page, 31.

The Vileda Vadrouille Twist Mop[12], with its special wringer and <u>long handle</u>, is excellent for cleaning the bath tub and kitchen, bathroom floors.   No need to bend or squat.

Beds, heavy sofas, cleaning equipment, etc. are easier to handle if they are on wheels.

When I have to bend or kneel I support myself with a kneeler stool or some similar device, page 27.

We replaced the lower kitchen cupboards with deep and wide drawers. It is easy to select utensils and at the same time stay off the knees. I lean on the counter when removing utensils from the bottom drawer.

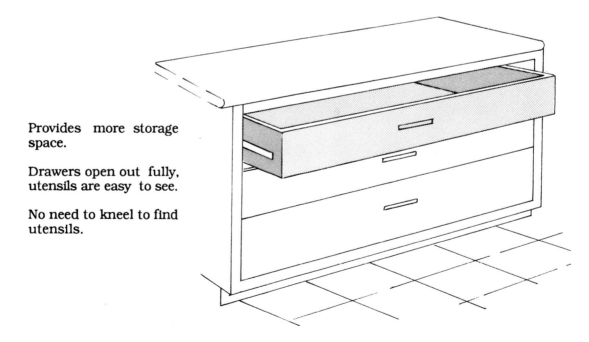

Provides more storage space.

Drawers open out fully, utensils are easy to see.

No need to kneel to find utensils.

Garden tips

The Arthritis Centre suggested these sources for information on handicapped gardener techniques:

> Gardening Techniques,
> Titchmarch, Alan.   Simon and Schuster, 1981.
>
> Some Tips and Tools for Elderly and Handicapped Gardeners
> Mother Earth News, May/June, 1984.

I found the following in the local library:

> Gardening for the Physically Handicapped and Elderly
> Mary Chaplin, in association with the Royal Horticultural Society
> B. T. Basford Ltd, 1978.

Our approach is to make our gardening easier and less work.

We use raised beds because they are easy to maintain and reduce the need for us to bend.

The middle of the bed is easy to reach from either side.

Intensive gardening and mulching reduces weeds.

One raised bed has a wide wooden edge on which we sit while weeding.

We gather leaves with a leaf blower and then shred them with other garden refuse for either mulching or composting.

> Mulching saves us a lot of time and energy. We apply it at least once a year, roughly 7-8 cm (3"), on any areas of bare ground. It controls weeds, breaks down and nourishes the plants.
>
> We mulch acid-loving plants such as rhododendrons with freshly shredded oak leaves, for others we use composted leaves.

Our rockeries are heavily mulched, planted with heathers and plants which also help in crowding out unwanted growth to further reduce maintenance.

We use containers for plants such as azalea, hibiscus, hydrangea, etc. and move them by handcart to different locations, to storage when dormant, for display when blooming.

Types of equipment we use:

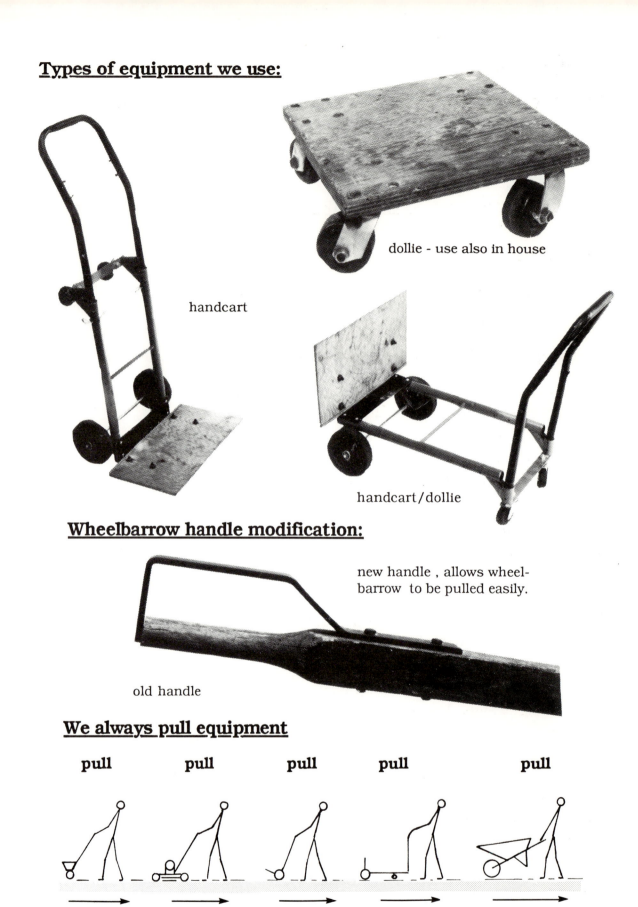

dollie - use also in house

handcart

handcart/dollie

Wheelbarrow handle modification:

new handle, allows wheelbarrow to be pulled easily.

old handle

We always pull equipment

pull   **pull**   **pull**   **pull**   **pull**

spreader   mower   handcart   dollie   wheelbarrow

Pulling this equipment backwards on level ground or up a slope is fine for my legs and hips and does not give me a problem with my osteoarthritis.

The added effort of pulling the equipment actually seems to increase those benefits which I feel from walking backwards.

Using garden tools properly is most important as is their design and type of construction.

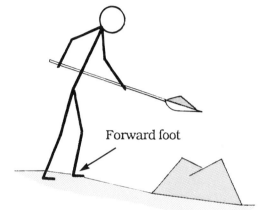
Forward foot

Long handled tools reduce the need to bend. I use a shovel with a small scoop to lift light loads.

When moving a load on a shovel I turn from the feet, point the forward foot in the direction of the turn to reduce twisting my body.

I move slowly making a small turn.

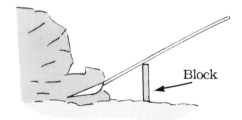
Block

When turning a compost heap or preparing a bed, I find it easier on my back and legs to use a block as a fulcrum and press down on the handle of the spade or fork rather than to lift the arms and back muscles.

The electric edge trimmer, using nylon line as a cutting tool, is a real boon for people like me. With it, I do not have to bend when trimming lawn edges and other unwanted plant growth.

I find a leaf blower mentioned on page 31 to be an important tool. My wet/dry vacuum is also useful for minor garden cleanup.

I quit before I get tired

Aches and pains are a warning that I am holding a position too long and fatigue results from any prolonged, continuous contraction of muscles.

If my memory were better I could save a great number of steps and I would not have to go back to get something I need here but left there.

<u>Forgetfulness may be an indication that I am getting tired.</u>

THE TRAGER ® EXPERIENCE[7]

I found the 18 months of the exercise program to be unrelieved hard work. If my condition were to be improved further, I was convinced it could only be through deeper mental and physical relaxation. I was not sure how I could achieve that.

I had practised some yoga for many years but had lost interest in it and had no wish to add it to a major exercise program. When I mentioned yoga and a need for deeper relaxation my chiropractor suggested I try Trager. I made an appointment.

> I relaxed on a massage table, lying either on my back or stomach, while a Trager practitioner gently shook, stretched and rhythmically rocked the muscles and joints in my legs, feet, arms, hands, back and neck for over an hour.
>
> A sense of deep relaxation gradually developed while the practitioner worked and asked me those questions which I now ask myself:
> ### *does it feel right, does it feel light?*
>
> While on the table I was not aware of the extent of that physical manipulation but when I got up I realized it had been thorough.

It was a feeling of deep relaxation, muscles pleasantly tingling, the sort of mental and physical state reached after playing hard, after a hot shower with a rubdown and a quiet rest.

> However, there was a difference because at no time had I physically exerted myself. All muscles had been relaxed while the shaking, stretching and rocking went on. I could not have obtained these results by myself. My muscles would have had to work, tightening up as I forced my limbs into desired positions, to cause tension which would have limited my movements.

With Trager work I have found my joints respond with a wider range of motion, muscles seem to flex in a more supple manner. I have successfully applied the Trager principles in modifying six of my own daily exercises.

This gentle treatment is something which I need to help me maintain a better mental and physical condition, to bend and move easily. What I learn from Trager stays with me. For further information, I suggest reading pages 37, 38, 40, 62, 71, and 73 or Dr. Trager's new book[13].

To paraphrase the song in <u>Mary Poppins</u>, "a little bit of Trager helps the exercises go easier."

EXERCISES

My reasons for exercising

The exercises which I perform are based upon those which were first selected for me by physiotherapists. Their purpose is:

- to increase muscle strength,
- to extend a joint's range of motion,
- to maintain a better physical condition,
- to ensure that body parts are activated daily.

I also use Dr. M. Trager's Mentastic^{SM} movements to stretch muscles and to reduce tension. These are detailed in his book Trager Mentastics: Movement as a Way to Agelessness[13].

Tailoring the exercises to my needs

Sometimes the advice of the experts falls short of my needs. I am not being critical, it is just that I need more than they seem to understand.

> Muscle strengthening is hard work but it is relatively straightforward applied mechanics. Increasing the range of a joint's motion, loosening up joints and muscles, is more difficult for me.

After my introduction to Trager® I began to study closely what was happening when I performed range of motion exercises.

> I concluded that I was being forced to stress related muscles when moving and rotating stiffened joints. Nothing seemed to be relaxing or to "feel right." I thought these movements should be pleasant to perform.

When there is tension in certain muscles during Trager work, the practitioner will tell me to relax, to let her take over so that she can work on the problem. I now recognize the extent to which my muscle tension inhibits movement of my joints.

To "feel right" I decided that I had to modify hip exercises, add others, to give myself a more relaxed exercising situation somewhat similar to that which is achieved in Trager work.

> I modified or introduced exercises 13, 15B, 16B, 17, 18, 19, and 31 because of the Trager® influence.

I look forward to the exercises now with a feeling that they are "right". The results have been positive, the feeling is "light", the movements are more pleasant to perform.

Performing these seven modified or new exercises on a daily basis has enabled me to reaffirm the information which is imparted to my body during each Trager ® work. The improvements have been quite outstanding and have been noticed by Maureen Jarvis during a session.

> After five months of Trager work and three months of these exercises, movement in both hips has greatly improved, the right hip has almost the freedom of "an eighteen year old!", while the battered old one on the left is now moving quite freely.

Exercises and my back

Early in my program some exercises caused a slight lower back ache for the first time in my life. I stopped doing them until my back recovered, hung my legs over the arm of a chair as shown on page 7, started up the exercises again slowly.

Over the past two years there have been no further problems and I have added back exercises and practised proper body mechanics, posture, etc. to keep my back in better condition.

Dr. Harwijne suggested that I include A Note for Back Pain Sufferers as shown on page 61.

Hydrotherapy

An enjoyable part of the Arthritis Centre's therapy was the hot pool, where the water was body temperature above 33° C (90° F).

It was suggested that the hydrotherapy be continued but unfortunately the public swimming pools are too cold for me, the warmer pools for children are too shallow. I would like to swim but I suffer pain from the colder water which causes cramps. Some pools are sectioned off and are not always easy to climb in and out off.

My approach to exercising

The exercises are performed with a physical and mental approach as noted below:

- I use a hot, quick shower to loosen muscles and joints.

- I know what exercises I want and I do what I feel that I need.

- I never allow any exercise to become a "1,2,3,4,5 times! Done! What is left to do? I can quit!" kind of activity.

I try not to count the number of times I move a limb during an exercise, however, I suggest 5 times might be my average. I was told stretching exercises should be held for at least 8 seconds.

I believe that effective muscle response may be determined without clocks or counting for a more restful control.

Instead I concentrate on the feeling in the joint or muscle. To me the real purpose of an exercise is how it helps me, how the exercised part feels, not the number of times that I do it.

I would like to emphasize that I never carry on with an exercise when pain develops, even if it is an exercise which I have done thousands of times before.

There always is a reason for pain and its cause must be determined quickly. One cause for me when exercising is overheating from too much clothing.

The exercises which I do

The exercises on the following pages are simply those which suit me. This is a rough index as to what parts of my body I find are affected by certain exercises:

Ankles:	Nos. 3A, 3B
Back:	Nos. 2, 6, 7, 19, 25, 26
Fingers:	Pages 58, 59, 60
Hips:	Nos. 1, 3C, 6, 8, 9, 10, 11, 12, 13, 15A or B, 16A or B, 17, 18, 19, 20, 22, 24, 25, 26, 27, 28, 31
Legs:	Nos. 1, 3C, 14, 19, 21, 23, 25, 26, 27, 28, 29, 30, 32
Neck:	Page 57
Shoulders	Nos. 4, 5

The back, legs and hips may all be involved during a specific exercise.

Frequency with which I do the exercises

I read that infrequently performed exercises are ineffective. In trying to get a better response from my joints it became apparent to me that regular exercise was important and I endeavour to perform my exercises **every day**.

If, for some reason, I am unable to perform the whole exercise program I skip the muscle strengthening ones and do only those which involve stretching and joint rotation.

Each individual has to learn his or her own exercise requirements, to find out:
- what helps and eases discomfort,
- when is the best time to perform the program,
- how to obtain the most benefit.

The experts emphasize individual diagnosis and exercise recommendations before starting an exercise program. I agree but, after that has been established, my experience indicates that the worth of any particular exercise should be assessed by the person performing it.

For what it is worth, I have timed myself lately and find that I spend close to 40 minutes on exercises every morning.

> The group of hip exercises with the leather straps, numbers 15B, 16B, 17, 18 and 19 take about 12 minutes. They are so effective I intentionally spend more time on them.

That does not mean that I rush the other exercises. They all have to be performed <u>gently</u> and <u>conscientiously</u> to be of any use.

I try to perform 14 selected Trager Mentastics ^{SM} movements for about 10 minutes on most evenings and find they are a good way to "wind down". These movements are not shown but photocopies of illustrations are available from a Trager practitioner. I quite enjoy one item entitled <u>Cosmic Dance</u>.

> I just turn on easy listening music and dance by myself. After a few trial movements "all joints seem to be on go".

> Who knows? I may yet dance with a partner again! This would be the real proof of my comeback and a happy day for me!

A total of 50 minutes of exercises per day seems to me to be a very small allocation of my time to ensure a happier, more comfortable life ahead.

EXERCISE NO. 1

Benefit to me:
 * hips, knees and leg muscles

I stretch each leg 4 - 5 times.

counter height
roughly 76 cm
or 30"

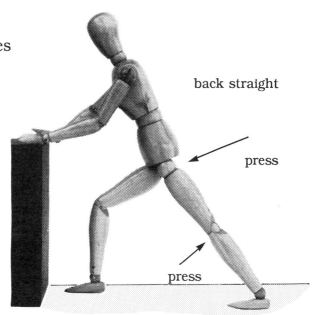

back straight

press

press

both feet flat on floor

EXERCISE NO. 2

Benefit to me:
 * Keeps my back feeling loose

I gently bend back and forwards 3 - 4 times.

hands on top of head

bend backwards

See page 61

bend knees slightly

keep feet apart

drop head and bend forward

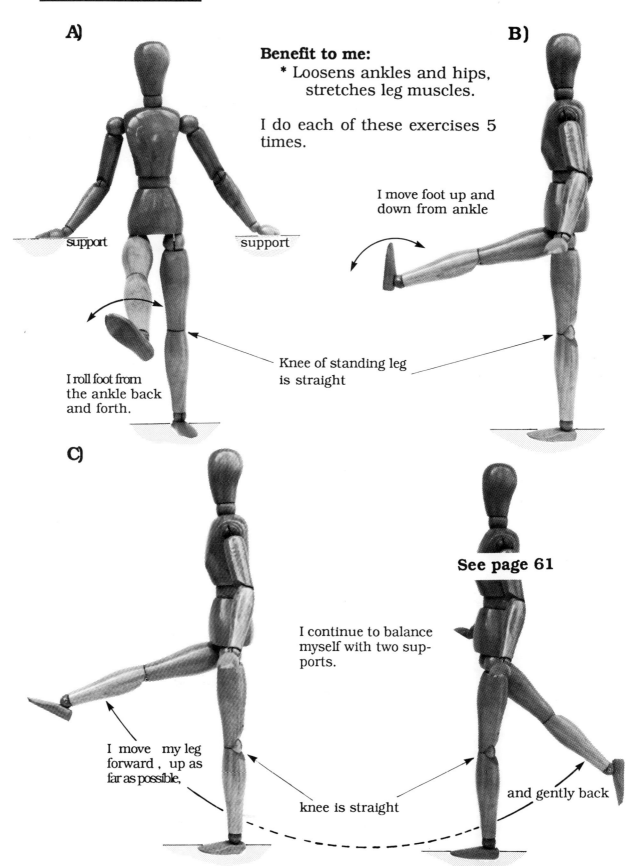

EXERCISE NO. 4

Benefit to me:
* Loosens shoulder muscles

I swing both arms together in a circle 5 times.

feet apart

EXERCISE NO. 5

Benefit to me:
* Loosens shoulder muscles.

I swing arms 5 times.

start swing

finish swing

feet apart

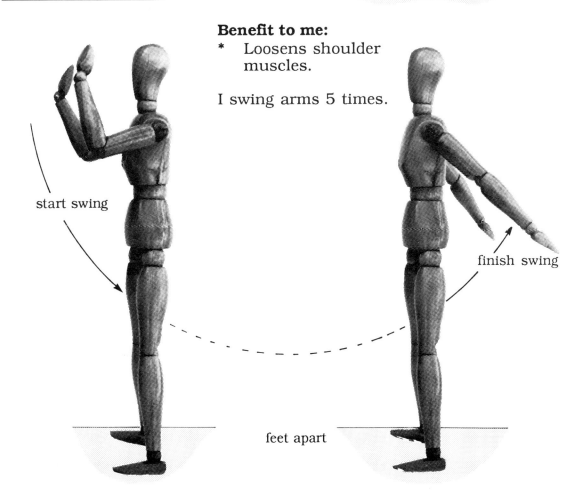

EXERCISE NO. 6

Benefit to me:
  * Loosens back and hips.

I bend to right and left 5 times.

I bend from the waist, slide my hand down my thigh as far as possible.

Knees straight

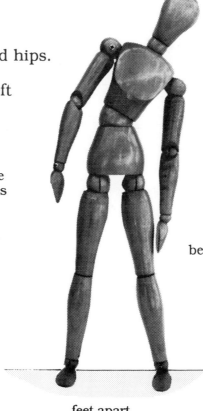

bend left

bend right

feet apart   feet apart

EXERCISE NO. 7

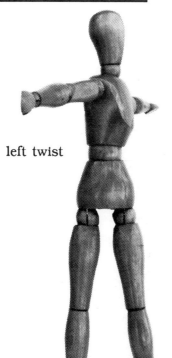

left twist

feet apart

Benefit to me:
  * Loosens back.

I twist upper body 5 times to left and to right.

arms straight, level with shoulders.

twist upper body from hips as far as possible

knees straight

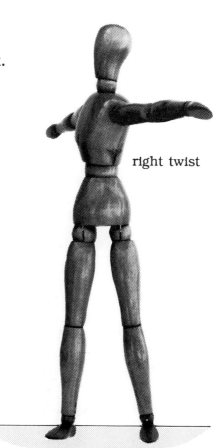

right twist

feet apart

EXERCISE NO. 8

Benefit to me:
* Increases range of motion of hips.

I swing legs apart 10-20 times.

Basic position on edge of table.

I keep back straight.

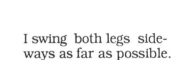

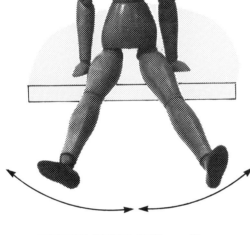

I swing both legs sideways as far as possible.

I use a table with height of 74 cm (29")

EXERCISE NO. 9

Benefit to me:
* Good hip exercise.

I lift legs alternately 10 times.

I sit straight and do not lean back.

I lift each leg alternately, bending at the knee and hip, bringing each knee up close to the chest.

EXERCISE NO. 10

Benefit to me:
* Loosens muscles around the hip area.

I shake and rotate each foot at least 30 - 40 times.

Knee of standing leg is straight.

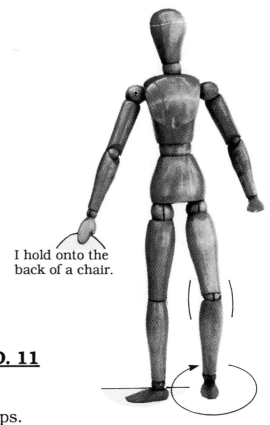
I hold onto the back of a chair.

shake, rotate foot

EXERCISE NO. 11

Benefit to me:
* Loosens hips.

I swing alternate legs sideways 5 times.

Knee of standing leg is straight.

support
swing

EXERCISE NO. 12

Benefit to me:
* Loosens hips.

I rotate alternate legs from the hips 5 times clockwise, then repeat anticlockwise.

Knee of standing leg is straight.

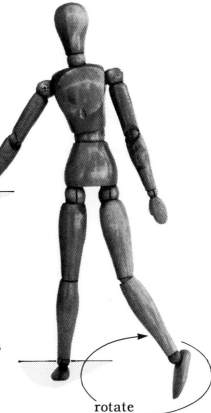
support
rotate

EXERCISE NO. 13

I perform this exercise lying on the floor or while standing on a thin plywood platform as shown on the right. I like the standing position, it is easy to perform and I obtain a good range of motion with my foot.

I roll the legs while holding each heel in place.

I stand on a thin plywood platform with one foot behind the vertical crosspiece, the other foot in front and its heel against the crosspiece.

Benefit to me:
 * Increases range of hip motion.

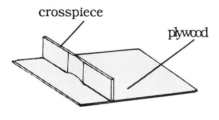

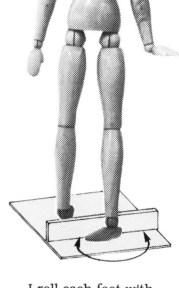

I roll each foot with the heel against the crosspiece.

EXERCISE NO. 14

Benefit to me:
 * Stretches leg muscles.

I pull back the toes with leg muscles, hold for count of 15, do this 5 times.

pull toes back

head on floor, with chin held down onto chest.

back of knees pressed down

NOTE: I prefer to use the straps, page 65, for exercises 15, 16, 17 and 18. I am careful not to pull too hard on the straps and possibly stress my shoulders from this action.

EXERCISE NO. 15

Benefit to me:
* Loosen hips and stretch muscles.

A) <u>Conventional way</u>:

I slide one leg sideways 20 times and repeat with other leg.

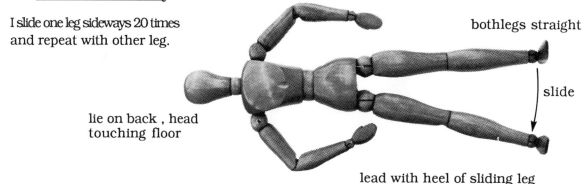

bothlegs straight

slide

lie on back, head touching floor

lead with heel of sliding leg

B) <u>Using the straps</u>

I relax leg muscles, pull one leg into a partially raised position, slightly higher than the other leg. With most of the leg's weight on the strap I move the strap to assist in bringing the leg back and forth.

Right leg being swung to my right side.

Right leg swung over to my left side.

- 48 -

EXERCISE NO. 16

Benefit to me:
* Increase hip's range of motion.

A) <u>Conventional way</u>

I pull with my hands (under the knees at "X") on alternate legs and bring each knee close to my chest 10 times.

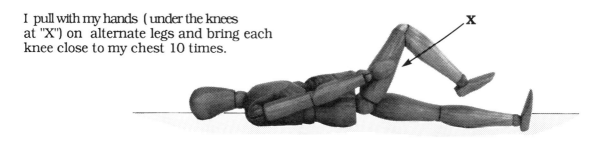

head on floor 　　back pressed 　　back of knee
(chin close to chest) 　　to floor 　　pressed down

B) <u>Using the straps</u>

I assume the same position. My leg muscles are relaxed, not assisting in any upward movement of the leg. This relaxed condition is more effective in developing a good range of motion for my hip.

Using both hands on one strap handle, I pull one leg up from its extended position towards and as close to the chest as possible. I hold the position for possibly 20 seconds, and repeat with the other leg, performing the exercise once - - a second time if it feels necessary.

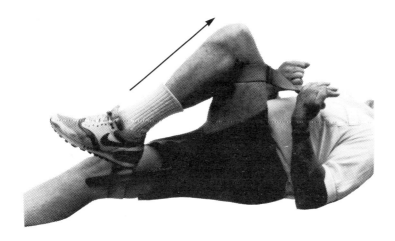

Note: I keep elbows on floor while doing exercises 15, 16, 17, and 18.

EXERCISE NO. 17

Benefit to me:
* increases range of hip's motion.

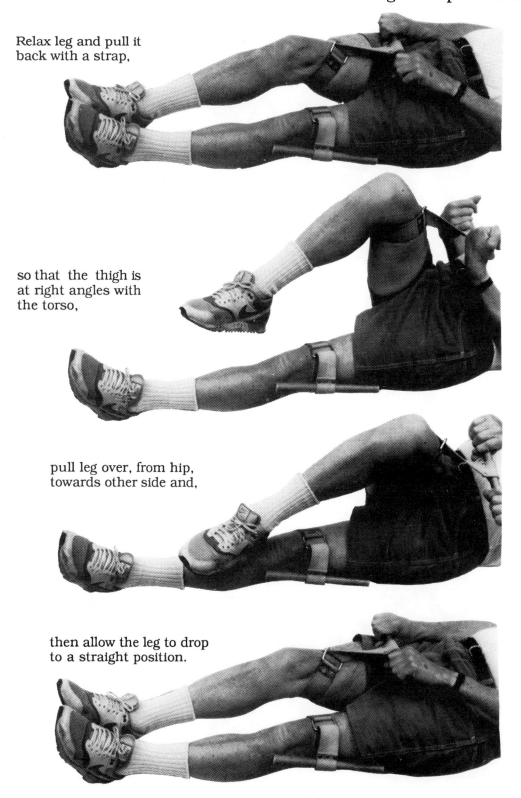

Relax leg and pull it back with a strap,

so that the thigh is at right angles with the torso,

pull leg over, from hip, towards other side and,

then allow the leg to drop to a straight position.

I perform this movement gently 7 times with each leg.

EXERCISE NO. 18

Benefit to me:
* increases range of hip motion

I do this 10 times with each leg.

2) The lower part of the leg is then twisted gently out to the side and then inwards across the body.

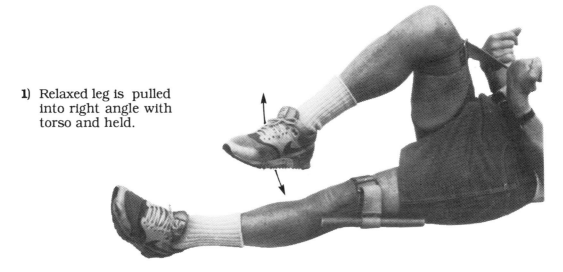

1) Relaxed leg is pulled into right angle with torso and held.

EXERCISE NO. 19

Benefit to me:
* loosens hip joint effectively, stretches leg, back muscles.

Note: I am now able to move this leg sideways, to the left and right, while it is raised.

I do this once or twice only.

Pull leg back as far as possible. Other leg remains close to floor.

two straps joined together.

I let the knee straighten out and relax the foot and leg muscles while pulling on the strap. For more effect, I place the strap over my head, hold it secure and pull by forcing my head back.

I hold for 20 seconds then lower the leg slowly with strap. Repeat with with other leg.

This leg remains on floor.

EXERCISE NO. 20

I do this 5 times with each leg.

Benefit to me:
* Increases hip movement.

Bend knee and force heel as close to buttocks as is possible.

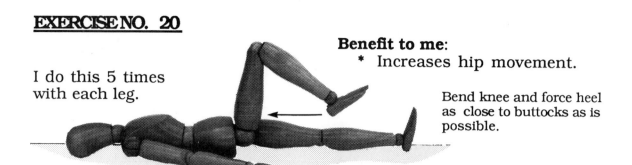

I keep this leg straight on floor.

EXERCISE NO. 21

Benefit to me:
* Strengthens leg and hip muscles.

I raise each leg, hold for count of 5 and repeat 5 times.

comfortably bent knee

5 cm (2")

I keep this leg straight and raise heel.

EXERCISE NO. 22

Benefit to me:
* Loosens muscles around the hip.

I roll bent leg back and forth at least 10 times and repeat with other leg.

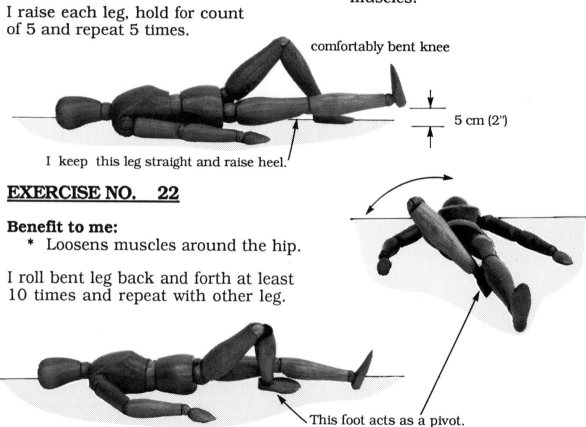

This foot acts as a pivot.

EXERCISE NO. 23

Benefit to me:
* Strengthens thigh muscles

I raise each leg alternately.

See page 61

I also use weights on the ankles.

EXERCISE NO. 24

Benefit to me:
* Exercises the hips.

I raise each leg alternately, hold for count of 5, repeat 5 times.

See page 61

keep legs straight   hold leg up for count of 5

hips must <u>not</u> lift off floor   one leg lies straight on floor

EXERCISE NO. 25

Benefit to me:
* Stretches leg muscles and those around the hips.

The following sketches show my progression in two months from:

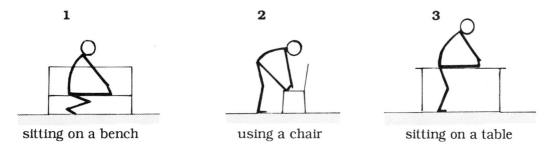

1 — sitting on a bench
2 — using a chair
3 — sitting on a table

bend forward

I now do the exercise as shown. I take a deep breath, exhale while pulling on toes, hold and another deep breath, etc. Change to other leg.

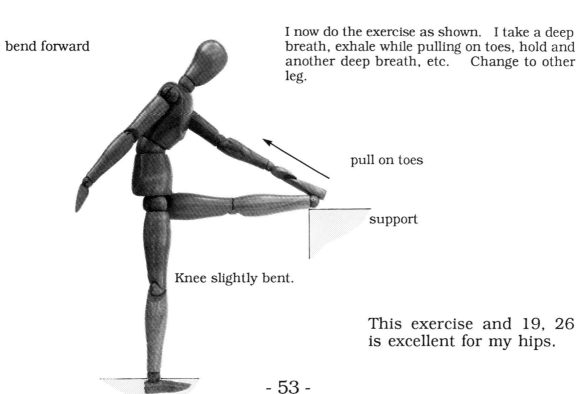

pull on toes

support

Knee slightly bent.

This exercise and 19, 26 is excellent for my hips.

- 53 -

EXERCISE NO. 26

Benefit to me:
* Stretches muscles in lower back, hips and back of thighs.

I bend over 10 times, alternating the position of my feet each time.

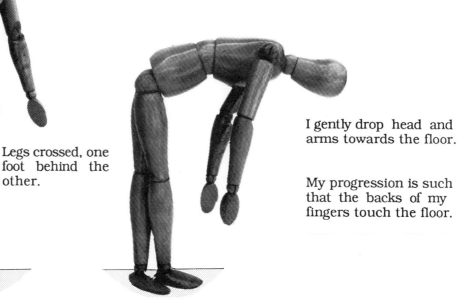

Legs crossed, one foot behind the other.

I gently drop head and arms towards the floor.

My progression is such that the backs of my fingers touch the floor.

EXERCISE NO. 27

Benefit to me:
* Strengthens leg muscles, flexes hip muscles.

I push ankles together 20 times.

1. I cross one ankle over the other.

Points 2 and 3 are important:

2. I sit on my hands which are tucked under each thigh.

3. I keep knees tightly together.

I push my ankles together, alternatively crossing one over the other.

I sit on a wooden or firm chair.

- 54 -

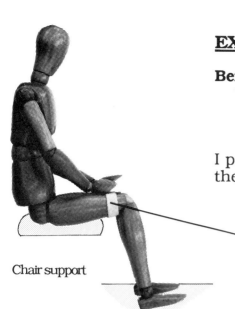

EXERCISE NO. 28

Benefit to me:
* Strengthens thigh and hip muscles, eases hip area stiffness.

I push knees sideways against the belt 20 times.

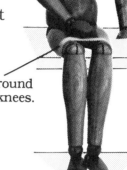

A belt is loosely fastened around around thighs just above the knees.

Chair support

EXERCISE NO. 29

Benefit to me:
* Strengthens thigh muscles.

Knees pressed together 20 times.

I sit on chair with hands between my knees as shown in the insert.

Hands act like springs taking up the thrust of my knees.

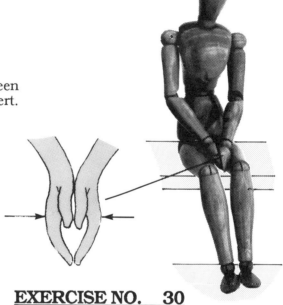

EXERCISE NO. 30

Benefit to me:
* Strengthens thigh muscles

Legs raised alternately 30 to 70 times.

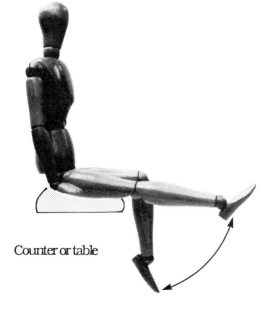

Counter or table

I raise one foot, bending at the knee. Raise and lower each foot slowly.

EXERCISE NO. 31

Benefit to me:
  * Increases range of motion of hip.

I move each foot sideways 20 times.

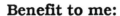
See page 61

I do not move this leg.

2.5 kg (5 Lbs.) ankle weights

I move this leg out and bend the knee.

I pivot on my knee to move my lower leg back and forth.

EXERCISE NO. 32

Benefit to me:
  * Strengthens leg muscles.

I raise each foot alternately.

ankle weights, each 2.5 kg (5 lbs.)

8 cm (3") block at back of knees.

I raise one foot at a time, hold, letting the block support the leg's weight.

This exercise combined with exercise 14 helps my hips.   I just pull back the toes of the supported leg with my muscles and hold.   I also pull in the stomach muscles while doing this and keep breathing normally.

EXERCISES I DO FOR MY NECK

To relieve neck pains some 25 years ago I was advised to do the following exercises gently <u>without sudden jerks</u>. I have performed them at least once a day and they have been effective.

A)

I flex my neck from side to side, moving the side of my head down to a shoulder and then down to the other shoulder.

I do this 5 times, slowly, gently, with no fast, sudden movements.

B)

I turn my head to one side, moving my chin in line with the shoulder, then I turn my head to the other shoulder.

I do this 5 times, slowly, gently, with no fast, sudden movements.

C)

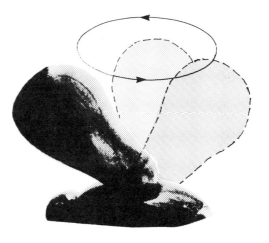

I move my head in a circular manner, as far to the side, back and front as is possible, flexing the chin down onto the chest as it passes.

I do this 5 times, slowly and gently.

For many years I have also gently flexed my head forward to my chest and then backwards. I mention this with caution as this exercise seems to be in some dispute amongst the experts at the present time.

EXERCISES I DO FOR MY FINGERS

For strengthening the fingers and improving muscle tone in the hands I do these exercises at least once a day, usually while I am lying on my back doing exercises 13 or 14 on page 47.

A)

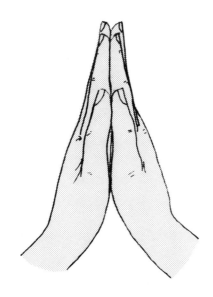

I press fingers, thumbs and palms of one hand firmly against those of the other hand.

Fingers and thumbs on each hand are held close together.

B)

I press the fingers and thumbs of one hand against those of the other hand with the thumbs extended as shown.

Fingers on each hand are held close together.

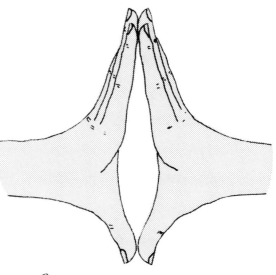

C)

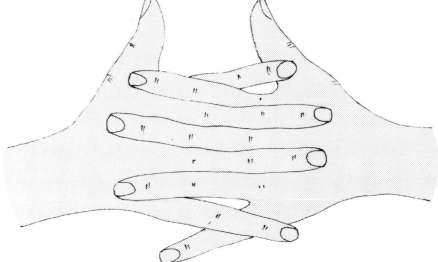

I bend my hands backwards, fingers pressing on the backs of the hands.

D)

I bend back the fingers of one hand with the other hand as shown.

E)

I pull my fingers down hard from the middle knuckle. My thumbs are forced into a similar bent position.

Then I straighten out fingers and thumbs, stretching them far apart.

F)

I press thumbs together while my fingers are interlaced.

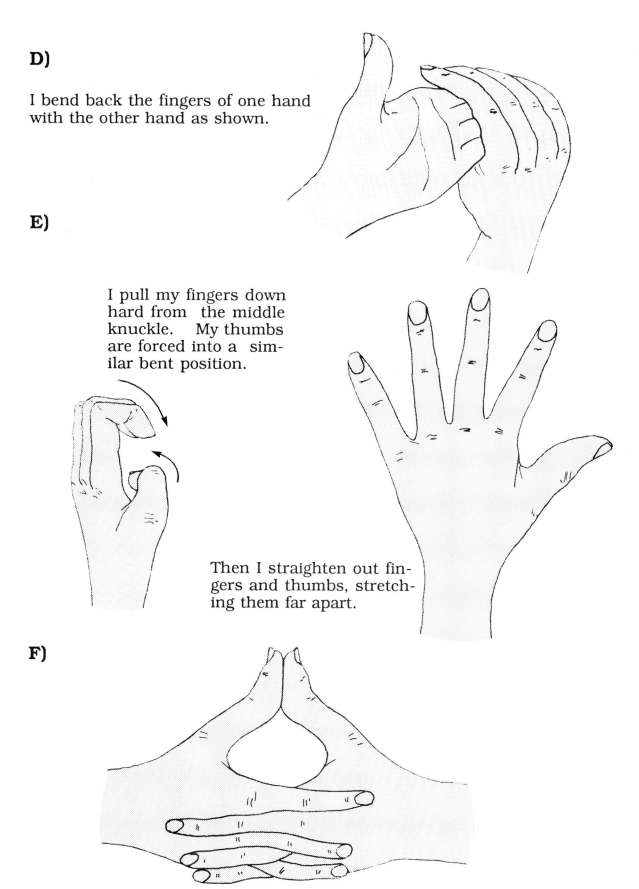

G)

I move my fingers and thumbs into a position as shown as if to grasp a rod of 5 cm (2") diameter tightly.

I hold this position briefly.

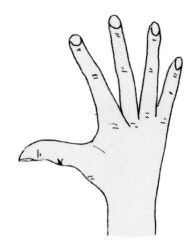

I then straighten and spread fingers and thumbs far apart, relax them and bring them together. Repeat 5 times.

H)

I stand erect, on my toes, and shake both hands vigorously until I can feel all the fingers becoming alive and the blood circulating strongly through them.

Note:

I find that finger exercises A, B, C and F are best done close to my chest, in a manner similar to the East Indian namasti. It seems to me that this position and those exercises help my arm muscles, especially those affected by "tennis elbow".

A NOTE FOR BACK PAIN SUFFERERS

I would like to emphasize that I do not have a back problem and, therefore, it is quite possible that:

> **Parts of my program may be totally unsuitable for those persons who suffer from osteoarthritis of the back or from other back malfunctions.**

Some of the exercises caused me temporary back aches at the start of my exercise program as noted on page 38.

My preferred sitting posture, discussed on pages 5, 21 and 28, contradicts the general recommendations of medical doctors, chiropractors and physiotherapists for back pain relief.

My knee joints will ache if I keep them bent for a prolonged period of time, therefore, I try to keep them as straight as possible. My hip joints also object to being "folded up" in an acute angle.

Lying on my stomach, page 5, was recommended by a physiotherapist, for up to 10 minutes daily. Some experts warn that this position accents the curvature of one's back and will create serious back problems. The way in which I do it seems to be comfortable and relaxing for me.

Placing a cushion under my stomach, as recommended to reduce back stress, makes my hips ache. On the other hand, I believe that stress may be reduced for me by lying on my stomach with my arms by my sides, shoulders down on floor and head turned sideways with cheek to floor.

Some of the exercises for the hips may cause stress in parts of the back and possibly should be avoided. I refer to exercises 3C(the backward swing), 23, 24, and 31. Note that The Arthritis Society regards these and also no. 2 as potentially dangerous.

My personal opinion is that all persons, even those with healthy backs, should not attempt these positions or perform any exercises without first obtaining professional advice.

> However, I believe that knowing one's own body is most important. One should recognize one's own limitations, understand personally what **feels right**, and not become too dependent upon a third party.

> In any event all exercises should be done gently to avoid straining muscles and ligaments. If a movement or position hurts, my reaction is to avoid the cause of the aches or pains immediately.

LOOKING BACK A FEW YEARS

Knowing what I know now,

I know that I would have made better progress had I been aware of:

<u>first</u>, Trager ®, how its mental, physical effects would make me more receptive to physiotherapy, exercising, walking, etc.

<u>second</u>, my physical need for special shoes, orthotics, orthopaedic seat and back supports, a foam mattress,

<u>third</u>, the additional discomforts caused by poorly designed seats, chairs and mattresses, from certain foods, my posture, hot and cold conditions and so forth.

With osteoarthritis we all seem unbelievably ignorant of what we need, of anything which will help us. I wish that the above information had been readily available to me some years ago.

I can not help but think that if I had developed this overall approach in 1983 the spread of osteoarthritis would have been effectively stopped and my joints would be in relatively good condition today. Considering what I have achieved since July, 1985 I would suggest that this is not just wishful thinking.

An objective look at my problems

I realize now that four to five years ago my body was showing signs of the developing osteoarthritis such as:
- discomfort in the form of aches, stiffness and cramping,
- difference in ways of reacting to people and situations,
- lowering of levels of energy and vitality,
- changes in carriage, and so forth.

Exercising and walking was a challenge all the time and I thought at least the latter should have been enjoyable.

A) In the beginning

When I began the physiotherapy and the exercise program, I was aching, tense and stiff, walking as a cripple might. The exercise program was hard work and yet it did not give me the overall relief which I needed.

Two years ago the chance of achieving my present improved condition seemed to be very remote.

B) The discomfort caused by my lack of knowledge

With osteoarthritis one expects to have continuing discomfort but my lack of knowledge made me suffer pain which I know now was totally unnecessary.

4 months of leg pains before I learned about jogging shoes.

15 months of other leg pains before I found the Obus Forme ® orthopaedic seat and back supports.

18 months of hip pains before I got the benefit of orthotics.

21 months of tension before I learned about Trager ®.

It is interesting to note that, while the use of these items greatly improved my wellbeing, I have not yet read about them in any book on arthritis. Even today few people know about Trager ® or all the orthopaedic supports which are available.

C) Hoping for the great cure-all

I wasted months looking for medicines, vitamins or diet supplements which would give relief from aches, pain and stiffness. I think that we are all conditioned to thinking that the medication approach will provide the great cure-all.

Then there are those who think that my diet must include copious quantities of apple cider vinegar or ripe cherries (Bings, Sweet Annes or just plain, old choke cherries all year round?). I often wonder what will be promoted next.

D) How about the individual's reponsibility?

Recently on a TV program for sore back equipment, etc. it was stated that in Norway the onus is more on the individual to improve one's own physical condition than it is in Canada.

In that respect, it was up to me to make changes in my way of living and to overcome much of the discomfort myself:

- regular exercising, at least 30 minutes every day,
- maintaining a balanced diet, low sugar, no alcohol,
- using proper body mechanics, correct posture,
- wearing proper clothing, using supports, and so forth.

Who is better qualified than I to know when it feels right?

AFTER ALL THIS, WHAT DO I RECOMMEND?

Mr. Jim Hume, columnist for the Victoria Times-Colonist calls arthritis "the best kept secret" yet 3.5 million Canadians have it.

> When I started to slow down I was not aware of what was happening to me and I meet people today who do not recognize the early arthritis symptoms in themselves.
>
> My earliest symptoms, 3 to 4 years ago, were leg pains, cramps, sore groin, swollen knees and stiff joints. At a recent Arthritis Centre building fund meeting I heard of a young woman who found that her persistent bad cold was a symptom of arthritis.

<u>First</u>, see your medical doctor immediately if you have :
- persistent pain and stiffness on arising.
- pain, tenderness or swelling in one or more joints.
- persistent pain and stiffness in the neck, hips, back or knees.

<u>Second</u>, make sure that you are referred to the Arthritis Centre when your doctor diagnoses arthritis.

> The Centre is the best place to start whether you are on medication or not. I watch the Victoria Centre's operations when I was receiving treatment. They do a lot of good for many people.

<u>Third</u>, try to keep active, exercise and walk.

> This is hard to do when pain dogs everything you might like to do. Recently Dr. G. A. May, M.D., said that the hardest part is to get older people to remain active and not become despondent.

<u>Fourth</u>, watch your diet.

> You may find as I did that certain foods literally mistreat your system. <u>You have to find this out for yourself</u> and act accordingly but personally I think that diet is very important.
>
> An American newspaper item reported that Dr. F. McDuffie[14] of the Arthritis Foundation indicated food poisoning had been "quite clearly" identified as a cause of reactive arthritis.

<u>Fifth</u>, don't tire yourself, don't undertake too much and don't move or carry something which is best trundled on a hand cart.

<u>Sixth</u>, find out what is **right** for yourself.

> It took me two years to find out what is right for me and I am still asking knowledgeable people for ideas.

EQUIPMENT I USE

My experience is that a quality product is always best and I have learned not to buy a product just because of price. With osteo-arthritis I need the most suitable shoes, mattress, seat and back supports, orthotics, etc. to help me.

I list what I consider to be the most important equipment.

Easi-kneeler stool (pages 27 and 73)

- Protects knees from stress when kneeling, getting down or up off the floor or ground and reduces the need for bending or squatting.

Exercise mat

- I use a large braided rug covered with a sheet instead of a mat.

- Provides protection when exercising on the floor.

Jogging shoes (pages 13, 14 and 72)

- Cushion the heel against shock when walking.

- Must have other recommended features.

Leather straps (pages 48, 49, 50 and 51

- Allow legs to be more relaxed when performing exercise nos. 15, 16, 17 and 18. Also by joining the two straps together it is possible to do exercise 19.

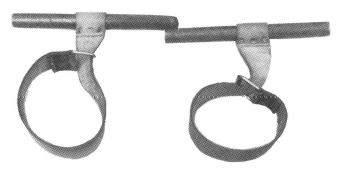

Foam Mattress (page 23)

- Provides vertical and lateral support to give a normal and more restful sleeping position reducing uncomfortable pressure points.

- Quality should be U28 extra, extra high density with medium firmness. Height of my mattress above the floor is roughly 64 cm (25") to protect my back and knees when getting up.

Moving Equipment (page 34)
- Permits heavy objects to be moved without stressing the body.

Seat and back supports (pages 22 and 69)
- Give positive support to buttocks and back for comfortable sitting in soft chairs, car, aircraft, bus, restaurant seats, etc.,

Orthotics (pages 15 and 70)
- Ensure correct support and create a more normal function of the feet and legs when walking or standing.
- I suggest that these must be more than sport shop, off-the-shelf arch supports.

Plywood Platform (page 47)
- Provides support for heel when performing exercise no. 13 in an erect position.

REFERENCES

1. **Arthritis and Exercise,
   A User's Guide to Fitness and Independence**

   Gwen Ellert, RN, BSN
   Published 1985 by Trelle Enterprises,
   305 - 1775 W. 10 Ave., Vancouver, B. C.   V6J 2A4

2. (reference pages 70- 71)

   **The Back Doctor
   Lifetime Relief for Your Aching Back**

   Dr. Hamilton Hall, M. D.
   Published 1983 by Seal Books,
   McCelland and Stewart-Bantam Limited,
   60 St. Clair Avenue East, Suite 601, Toronto, Ont.   M4T 1N5

3. (references page 2 and page 3, Arthritis News, Summer, 1986)

   Arthritis News is the official publication of The Arthritis Society and is published in March, June, September and December.

   The Arthritis Society,
   250 Bloor St. East, Suite 401, Toronto, Ont.   M4W 3P2

   The following is from an Arthritis Society Information Series:

   The Arthritis Society is the only agency in Canada devoted solely to the search for the causes and cures for arthritis - the country's number one chronic affliction.   Additionally, it is the prime resource for Canada's nearly 3.5 million arthritis victims for information and educational materials about the disease and has been, for more than 35 years, the leading sponsor and proponent of treatment and control measures.

   NATIONAL IMPACT
   The Society has had a national impact on arthritis since its formation in 1948 by a group of dedicated, far-seeing lay and medical professionals.   It presently has major divisions in every province and nearly 1000 branches and committees in communities across the country.   The value of this totally volunteer support network is impossible to measure, but without its energy and effort, much of what has resulted from the achievements of past years would not exist today.

   FUNDING
   A major and continuing task of the Society is to raise the funds necessary to support its research, manpower development, training and public education programs.   It does not receive any government support for these programs and must, as a consequence, depend on its volunteer force and the Canadian public.

   THE SITUATION TODAY
   Thirty-five years ago people with arthritis were considered prime candidates or the public wards and little, if anything, was known about how to diagnose, treat or control the disease.

In 1948, the year the Society was formed, there were only four rheumatologists (specialists in arthritis) in Canada. Today, thanks to the support of tens of thousands of Canadians who helped make their training possible, there are more than 180.

That same year, a person with severe arthritis could expect to spend a substantial portion of his or her life receiving in-hospital care. Today, early diagnosis, far more effective treatment programs, and a much clearer understanding of the evolution of the disease and its impact have reduced that need for expensive in-patient care to less than two weeks in all but the most serious of cases.

STILL AVAILABLE
That important in-hospital care is still available, of course, but ..... the majority of persons with serious problems can be treated on an out-patient basis .....

Gout, one of the most painful of arthritis can today be totally controlled. Lupus, a veritable death sentence 20 years ago, can now be successfully managed to a very large measure. Arthritis due to infection, a type capable of destroying a joint in some cases in less than a week, can now be quickly controlled. Juvenile arthritis has now been clearly identified as a specific malady with its own treatment and control methods.

THE ECONOMICS OF ARTHRITIS
Arthritis is a disease of staggering economic proportions. It affects nearly 15 percent of the population: one in seven people and one in three families.

Canada Health and Welfare statistics indicate that more than 1.4 million members of the work force have arthritis. Collectively, they lose more than 22 million work days per year because of their disease. The cost of this **alone** is more than 22 million lost man-days of production and more than $1.1 billion in lost wages! The cost to Canada in terms of lost tax income is nearly $150 million! The cost in terms of increased prices for goods and services is incalculable.

(Comment: With those figures one would think our politicians would show more interest in diverting some of our tax dollars from their less needy projects and try harder to help overcome arthritis).

4. **The Arthritis Society, B.C. Division**, is the Arthritis Society's office for British Columbia and the Yukon.

The B.C. Division, is a non-profit voluntary health agency; a leader in arthritis research, education and treatment programs. Funding comes from private donors, agency support and government grants.

Admission for treatment at a Centre is by a medical doctor's referral only.

The Arthritis Centre,
895 West 10th Avenue, Vancouver, B. C. V5Z 1L7
(604) 897-7511

The Victoria Arthritis Centre,
2680 Richmond Ave., Victoria, B. C. V8R 4S9
(604) 598-2277

5. **Obus Forme Ltd.** is the manufacturer of orthopaedic seat and back supports and other health care products. Since 1980 it has shipped thousands of back rests and seats to countries throughout the free world.

    Obus Forme's president, Frank Roberts, a former back pain victim, developed the unconventional spinal support during the late 70's working out of his garage at home and from the start business was brisk in meeting the demand.

    Other products which might be of interest to persons with osteoarthritis include Obus Forme Plus, a back support with heat, and a reusable Hot or Cold Compress.

    So far I have only tried the seat and backrest. The following information which I obtained from Obus Forme Ltd. gives a bit more detail for the reader.

    What does the SEAT do for me?

    Its contour seating properly aligns and supports my buttock providing necessary therapeutic *relief* from *sitting pressure*.

    In what way does the SEAT function to reduce my discomfort?

    It distributes upper body weight throughout the buttock region surrounding the ischial tuberosities (the bone protuberances of the buttock area, generally known as the "the sitting bones"). It forces the upper body to sit on the buttocks, reducing the stress that sitting places on the spine.

    I found the SEAT better than cushions and other seating which I had tried in the months prior to November, 1986. As I have noted it was the first to give me relief and I concur with the Obus Forme's reasoning which follows:

    1. It has a firm, flexible support providing a superior surface for the buttock to rest upon. Cushions and conventional seating allow "sitting bones" to sink into soft cushion-type seating. Its oblique angle depressions reduce uncomfortable point loads in the pelvis.
    2. Its contured sides relieve pressure on the bottoms or sides of the hips since these outermost bone projections of the hips *can* become very painful if they come under only slight pressure for long periods of time.
    3. The anal cut-out reduces pressure strain on bulging discs and worn facet joints in the lumbar spine.
    4. The raised pommel minimizes the incidence of leg spasms by separating the legs and preventing leg rotation.
    5. A concave space is provided under the thighs with no pressure to cause muscle fatigue, poor ciculation and possible pinching of nerves, with swollen ankles and feet.
    6. Adjustable seat depth (zip-out section) allows correct thigh support and proper knee clearance regardless of stature or build. Assures excellent lumbar/thoracic support, promotes unrestricted circulation.

    I can verify from actual use and close observation that the design and construction outlined in items 1, 2, 4, 5 and 6 definitely reduces pain and discomfort for me.

6. The foot devices which I obtained through my chiropractor are bio-mechanical devices commonly referred to as **orthotics**. Their design in the laboratory was based upon casts or impressions in Bio-Foam™ taken by my chiropractor.

   The following explanations of the role which your feet play while you walk and the reasons for using orthotics were obtained through the courtesy of a Toronto company **The Orthotic Group Inc.**

   The structure of your foot supports your entire weight. The slightest mis-alignment of muscles and bones can cause many different problems.

   The symptoms of faulty foot mechanics may begin with any of the following:
   1. localized foot pain
   2. bunions, hammer toes
   3. arch, heel pain
   4. leg, knee pain
   5. hip or back pain; even neck pain.

   Note: Item 5, hip pain, was my first indication that I needed orthotics.

   PROBLEM FEET MAY MAKE YOU CAN HURT ALL OVER !

   The Arthritis Centre or your chiropractor can examine you and prescribe foot orthotics, if they are necessary, to help correct your specific body imbalance.

   WHAT ARE PRESCRIPTION ORTHOTICS?

   Prescription orthotics are medical appliances that are custom made to correct abnormal foot and leg functions. They are made according to the diagnosis of your specific foot imbalance.

   Orthotics work on the feet in the same way braces work on the teeth - by exerting gentle consistent pressure to bring foot muscles and bones back into proper alignment.

   They fit comfortably in shoes and are usually made of flexible molded thermoplastic. The devices are always made from custom precise impressions taken of your feet.

   HOW DO ORTHOTICS HELP?

   Your feet are the foundation of your entire body. They do an incredible amount of work each day. The smallest imbalance can cause a great deal of discomfort, but properly fitted prescription orthotics help restore the normal balance and alignment of your body and bring relief from fatigue and pain. Orthotics are so comfortable, and help your feet work so naturally that you will want to wear them as much as possible.

   THE WEARING OF ORTHOTICS

   In your shoes your feet rest comfortably on the orthotics. Your feet are gently and consistently forced into the correct functioning position for walking, running and standing. Pressure points, improper rotation of the foot, painful muscle strain, and abnormal forces on the legs, hips and spine are eliminated because orthotics enable your feet to function properly.

7. **Trager** ® psychophysical integration and **Mentastic**^{SM} movement education are the discoveries of Milton Trager, M.D.

   He discovered that persons with polio damaged limbs, back and other pain causing problems would respond positively to a hands-on approach which involved a rocking, stretching and shaking of parts of the patient's body, and that people could maintain and enhance these positive results by doing the Mentastics movements on their own.

   He had been a successful therapist for 50 years before he attempted to teach others his approach and consequently he was able to offer an unusually refined and tested application.

   The physical movements of Trager work are mentally directed. In Dr. Trager's words:

   > My work is directed towards reaching the unconscious mind of the patient. Every move, every thought communicates how the tissue should feel when everything is right.

   > The mind is the whole thing, what has developed between the ears. That is all that I am interested in. You can keep the rest of it.

   > I am convinced that for every physical non-yielding condition there is a psychic counterpoint in the unconscious mind, and exactly to the degree of the physical manifestation.

   > Trager work consists of the use of the hands to influence deep-seated psycho-physiological patterns in the mind and to interrupt their projection into the body's tissue. The purpose of my work is to break up these sensory and mental patterns which inhibit free movement and cause pain and disruption of normal function.

   > The approach is to impart to the patient what it is like to <u>feel right</u> in the sense of a functionally integrated body-mind. Since the inhibiting patterns are affected at the source (the mind), the patient can experience long-lasting benefits. The result is general functional improvement.

   The Trager Institute,
   10 Old Mill St.,
   Mill Valley, CA 94941-1891.
   (415) 388-2688

8. **Walk-On**

   Stephen Kiesling, Senior Editor American Health Magazine

   E. C. Frederick, Ph.D., Nike Sports Research Laboratory

   Published by Rodale Press Inc.
   Copyright © 1986 by Nike, Inc.
   Nike, Inc. Public Information Office
   3900 SW Murray Blvd, Beaverton, OR 97005.

9. Design and construction details showing the differences between walking and running shoes.

These illustrations have been copied from the book Walk On[8] and are shown courtesy of Nike, Inc.

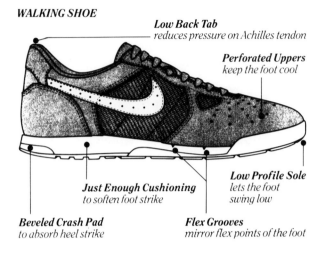
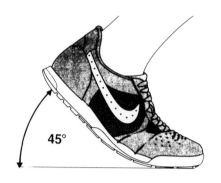
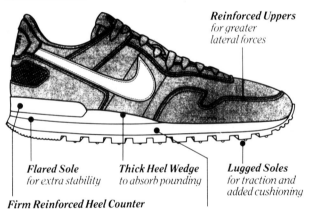

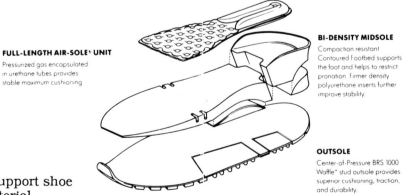

Details of the Nike Air ® Support shoe taken from advertising material.

10. Church pew dimensions, page 21.

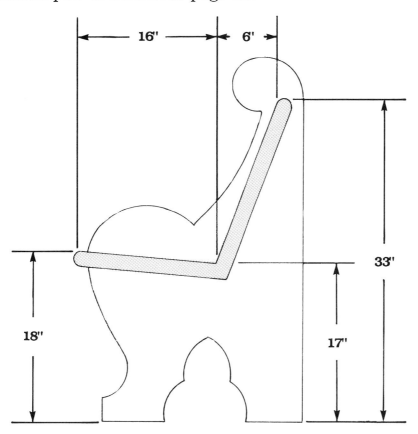

11. The **Corrie Easi-Kneeler Stool**, made by J. B. Corrie Limited of Petersfield Hants, England, is a practical and versatile aid for the garden or home as a kneeling mat or handy chair. Its sides enable a person to use the arms and push up when rising.

    It is constructed of tubular steel and finished in green enamel. It has a plywood kneeling base with a foam cushion which may be flipped over to provide a sitting surface.   Distributed by:

    Dominion Seed House,
    Georgetown, Ontario,
    L7G 4A2

12. The **Vileda Vadrouille Twist Mop**™ comes in a kit which includes a pail, wringer and mop. It is simple to use and eliminates the need to bend or kneel when washing floors. It is not necessary to bend over when using the wringer. Available at department, hardware stores and distributed by:

    F. P. Feature Products Inc.,
    Mississaugua, Ontario.

13. **Trager Mentastics: Movement as a Way to Agelessness**

   Dr. Milton Trager, M.D.
   with Trager Instructor Cathy Guadagno, Ph.D.
   Published 1987 by Station Hill Press,
   Barrytown, NY 12507

   Trager Mentastics is Dr. Trager's long-awaited publication on the essence of his teaching on Menatastics. The book includes materials taken directly from workshops as well as more than 100 photos of Dr. Trager and others doing the Mentastics movements. The book serves as a valuable source of support and inspiration in the use of Mentastics.

14. Dr. Frederic McDuffie, M.D.,
    Medical Director,
    Arthritis Foundation,
    1314 Spring St. N.W.,
    Atlanta, Ga 30309